SUPERNATURAL ARCHITECTURE

PREPARING THE CHURCH FOR THE 21ST CENTURY

by

STAN E. DEKOVEN, PH.D.

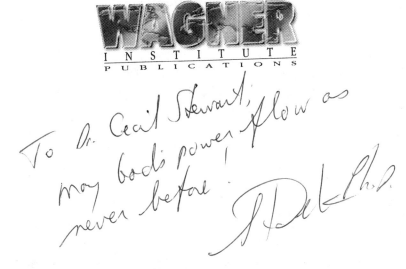

SUPERNATURAL ARCHITECTURE
PREPARING THE CHURCH FOR THE 21ST CENTURY

© COPYRIGHT 1997 by Stan E. DeKoven, Ph.D.

ISBN: 1-58502-001-X

All rights in this book are reserved worldwide. No part of this book may be reproduced in any manner whatsoever without written permission of the author except brief quotations embodied in critical articles or reviews.

For information on reordering please contact:

Wagner Institute Publications
11005 State Highway 83N, Suite 127
Colorado Springs, CO 80921
719-262-0442

All Scripture references are taken from the New American Standard Version of the Bible, used by permission.

Acknowledgments

It is with a heart full of thanksgiving that I gratefully acknowledge and bless the following family, friends and associates who have graciously contributed to my thinking and writing on this topic.

First, my beautiful bride Karen and wonderful daughters Rebecca and Rachel are a continual source of prayer and support to my work. Without them, life itself would be barely worth living.

Second, there are many pastors and teachers carrying an apostolic revelation who have throughout their lives and teachings stretched my understanding. These include Dr. G. Randolph Gurley, Rev. Lee Speakman, Dr. Ken Chant, Dr. Joseph Thornton, Dr. Doug Jarrard, Dr. Lee Stutzman, Rev. George Runyan, Dr. Bill Stafford, Dr. Kluane Spake, Dr. Jason Guerrero, Dr. A. L. Gill, Dr. John McGeorge, Pastor Marilu Dones Reyes, Dr. Apostle Luciano Padilla, Dr. Anthony Spero, Dr. David Wyns and my pastor and friend Dr. Joseph J. Bohac.

A special thanks to Apostle Dr. C. Peter Wagner for his friendship and kind foreword.

Finally to our wonderful staff at Vision, Maureen Kelley, Delores Horsman, Michelle Newton, Marcelo Romero, Cliff and Sheila Hogstrom. My many thanks, as well to Mr. Michael Wourms, one of the most gifted writers and editors in America today.

May the Lord help us all to build this Church...until He comes.

Foreword

For thirty years I have been a professor of church growth. One of my tasks has been to undertake the necessary research to answer the following four questions:
- Why does the blessing of God rest where it does?
- Since it is obvious that not all churches are equal, why is it that at certain times and in certain places some churches seem to be more blessed than others?
- Can any pattern of divine blessing on churches be discerned?
- If so, what are the salient characteristics of unusually blessed churches?

It has now become clear that at this particular point of history, the unusual blessing of God is resting on what I like to call churches of "The New Apostolic Reformation." This does not mean that God is not blessing some other churches as well. But it does derive from the fact that in virtually every part of the world the fastest growing group of churches are New Apostolic Churches.

Not everybody is aware that these churches even exist. Many who do realize it have discovered no way to infiltrate and understand the New Apostolic Churches. But my friend, Stan DeKoven is one who does. As the President of Vision International University, he has been deeply involved in training cutting-edge leadership for New Apostolic Churches.

Stan's fingerprints are all over these churches!

Supernatural Architecture is a book that has addressed the questions relating to the pattern of today's divine blessing, and the salient characteristics of the blessed churches. Stan accurately sees that the Church of the 21st Century will be the Church which exhibits these characteristics.

But he goes beyond that assessment.

Dr. DeKoven probes the reasons why New Apostolic Churches are such a driving force for the Kingdom, showing through careful research that they are, from their roots up, biblical churches. They adhere to the fundamental patterns established by God in the Old Testament and in the intertestamental period, and they also have been molded by the governmental pattern taught by Jesus and practiced by the apostles.

All this is to say that the book you hold in your hands can be regarded as a biblical theology of the New Apostolic Reformation. It goes hand-in-hand with other books describing this dynamic movement from empirical, sociological or methodological perspectives. I will be recommending Stan DeKoven's book to my students because I know it will build their confidence that the ways that they have come to understand as the Church are ways near to the heart of God.

As you read *Supernatural Architecture,* you will grow in your gratitude to God for the privilege of living in a generation to which God has given so much exciting revelation about the ways and means of advancing His Kingdom.

C. Peter Wagner, Chancellor
Wagner Leadership Institute
Colorado Springs, CO

Table Of Contents

Acknowledgments 3
Foreword 5
Introduction 9

Chapter One *Church Growth Reviewed* 15
Chapter Two *The Church From The Start* 31
Chapter Three *One Under God* 35
Chapter Four *According To Patterns* 45
Chapter Five *The Jesus Pattern I* 59
Chapter Six *The Jesus Pattern II* 75
Chapter Seven *The Jesus Pattern III* 81
Chapter Eight *The Mission Mandate* 95
Chapter Nine *The Downpour* 99
Chapter Ten *When Heaven Came Down: Crisis One* 105
Chapter Eleven *The Widow's Way: Crisis Two* 111
Chapter Twelve *The Barnabas Blessing-
  The Antioch Pattern* 119
Chapter Thirteen *The Ephesus Model* 135
Chapter Fourteen *The Church of the 21st Century* 157

Afterward 175
Appendix 1 183
Appendix 2 193
Bibliography 201
Recommended Resources 203
About The Author 205
Other Books By Dr. DeKoven 207

INTRODUCTION

As we approach the 21st Century, it behooves us as ministers of Christ to gaze again on the ministry of Jesus. In recent reflection, there are many things in Christ's ministry to hurting humanity which are noteworthy...too many to discuss here. However, in all His greatness, one dimension is often overlooked, especially by the evangelical and the charismatic ministers.

Scripture reveals that Jesus only did what His Father told Him to do...and that He be about doing good (God things), healing all oppressed of the devil, for God was with Him (Immanuel). In recognizing that Jesus acted on the Father's desire, doing the work He was called to do, we see an influential intent of immense importance.

Sin causes isolation.

Sickness causes isolation.

Mass choices in society create isolation.

Isolation and unfamiliarity create division, ignorance and blindness of soul, often institutionalized over generations (racism, ageism, sexism, Christian sin, etc., ad nauseum). The distinctiveness of Jesus' ministry can be seen in His incredible ability to bring Good News to poor souls, removing the barriers to social intercourse, opening wide the door to disenfranchised, isolated individuals and groups (including families) who were once far off, now brought near. Examples of this could fill volumes. A few instances will suffice.

Consider the leper in Matthew 1. Charismatics will concentrate on the power encounter and the miraculous healing wrought by the touch of the Master (see the woman with issue of blood). The more liberal theologians will see the humanitarianism of Christ while wondering why He did not establish Christ Hospital in Palestine.

But notice the greater intent of Christ's example.

In verse 4, after the leprosy was removed by the power of God, Jesus urges (commands) the man (him, not the former leper!) to *"show yourself to the priest and offer for your cleansing what Moses commanded (Lev. 14:1-32) for a testimony to them."*

How often I have read this passage while missing a key element. The offering to the priest, the testimony given was not to brag on God alone (or as in many charismatic circles, to brag on one's worthiness to receive, or God's good judgment in choosing me for a miracle, healing, or blessing) but also for the priest, as representative of the faith community, to acknowledge that isolationist treatment of the leper could no longer be given, and that acceptance into the community of faith was mandated.

The woman at the well (John 4:7-30) gives another example of Christ's ministry of wholeness. This woman was isolated and unacceptable to polite society; she could only draw water by herself, devoid of the fellowship of the other Samaritan women. Her healing of soul occurred through the revelation of Jesus as the Christ (the first one to receive it); He removed her shame and transformed her purpose, which led to national revival.

It has been justly stated that all brokenness occurs within relationship. Long before divorce there existed a happily married, hopeful couple. Prior to the alcoholic, drug addict, abuser or victim was a person, created in the image of God with infinite worth and potentiality. All brokenness can be traced to relational wounds found in family, society, religious articles, and directly with God himself, *"all have sinned and fallen short ...the wages of sin is death, or isolation from God..."* (Romans 3:23, 6:23).

Just as brokenness occurs through relationship, no healing will occur without it.

Two Remarkable Things

In all of Jesus' ministry, two things stand out to me, and are so vitally needed in the 21st Century. These two things seemed to resonate in Christ, and He responded to them with remarkable power, delight, faith and community.

Whenever Jesus found faith (expecting that a good God can and will act on our behalf), bells and whistles went off. The leper beseeching Him, the woman at the well engaging Him, children coming to Him, roofs removed for friends to get to Him, little men climbing trees to see Him, the young man who squandered his inheritance, returning still smelling of pig and whore, all had two things in common.

First, they were all marginalized people.

Some were rich, some poor, with differing cultures and races represented. All were wounded by relationships, and all were humble enough to admit they needed a savior.

Second, each expressed their faith in their own way.

Jesus, with true eyes of compassion, was able to look beyond their brokenness (causing isolation from community) and responded to faith with virtue (power/life). Unlike modern Church life (the worst example of which is the so-called "televangelist" who unknowingly encourages isolation. He says, "Send in your offering, touch your T.V. screen for a healing." (The process is all done with anonymity and isolation). Where much of the modern Church emphasizes miracles or healings, Jesus emphasized the return to community — a return which should have been in most cases unnecessary, and in rare cases resulted in full, complete and immediate restoration (see the Prodigal son).

Jesus understood (and so must we) that there is something much worse than being without eye or limb, or from one culture or another. Being separate from the Kingdom of God (the true Christian culture) is the only tragedy! Jesus ministered to the whole person, with a focus on returning to community those who, from a poverty of spirit, responded in faith to His message of hope — a message they believed without reservation.

Which brings me to a greater question... "What was it about Jesus that made it easy for the child, the leper, the prostitute, the tax collector, the embarrassed wedding host, etc. to come to Him?"

The answer is painfully obvious, but only the blind can see it.

Blind Jesus

Jesus was blind to leprosy; He did not see a leper, He saw a man.

Jesus was blind to the adulterer; He did not see the adultery, He saw a woman.

Children were not a nuisance, but the inheritors of the Kingdom.

There was no woman of Samaria, just a woman with thirst. No soldier with a sick daughter, just a father with a broken heart. What made Jesus so very approachable, and what seemed to release God's power through Him when faith was present, was the compassion He felt for the "whosoever will" of His day. What made Jesus so desirable, what seemed to release God's power through Him was manifested faith that triggered the compassion He felt for the common man.

The Church of the 21st Century must somehow return to the ministry of Jesus Christ!

We must acknowledge that brokenness is everywhere, and our incessantly morbid need to analyze the cause before providing the cure must close. Who cares (does God?) how the AIDS, cancer, divorce, homosexuality, came to be. If faith can be formed, we must look beyond the color, race, socioeconomic status, denomination or any other thing that divides us, seeing instead the wonderful person, created in God's image, in need of God's grace, to be administered to by God's servants, to open again (where wholeness will occur) to them the Christian community, the Kingdom of God. People knew Jesus saw beyond their label and was moved with compassion to call life from death, hope from despair, friendship from isolation.

The last thing Jesus taught before His death was the importance of community. In the Upper Room He washed the disciples' feet, showing humble servant-leadership to be a requirement for Kingdom service. He gave them the ritual meal, becoming the common bond for all believers throughout the ages, to be celebrated as often as we gather. He instituted in His apostles the vital truth that unity in love was/is the goal; all else is secondary to our vibrant love for one another.

Oh, how far we have struggled and how far we have to go!

We must return to the way of Christ!

Jesus built a community of faith which was to be inclusive (not exclusive as the Jews of His day, or the Romans, Greeks and many present cultural groups), motivated by love, invigorated by a level of faith in God's ample provision. His disciples took the ministry and methods of Jesus (in limited scope, according to their gifting, limited worldview, measure of faith) and applied them in their cultural context.

We, His ministers of the 21st Century, are challenged to do the same.

Chapter One

Church Growth Reviewed

There has been a strong emphasis on church growth strategy over the past several years, with differing results. Without a doubt, the motivation for church growth teaching and strategies has been to address the unfortunate reality of a stagnant Church in need of radical revival.

The church growth movement has been criticized by some as being too worldly, emphasizing "Madison Avenue" techniques and slick advertising schemes.

Though there are some advocates of the secularization of the Church to include market strategies and technological implementation as the answer to Church stagnation, most would not hold to this view. In fact, the evaluation of some that church growth experts are less than godly in focus and purpose is too harsh. There is much good which has come from the research and implementation in the Western church.

Yet, one cannot help but stop and evaluate what the church growth movement has truly accomplished. Most indications are that the church in the West is continuing to decline in both numbers and influence. At the same time, the church in the Two-Thirds World (South America, Africa, Asia and Eastern Europe) is expanding at a phenomenal rate, hardly assisted by any Western church growth strategy! Even the casual observer would assume there is something missing in the Western church that is alive and vibrant in the rest of the Kingdom of God. Perhaps there is much that one can learn from the church that lacks resources but has a demonstration of power.

One author and acute observer of the Two-Thirds World phenomena and church growth in general is Dr. C. Peter Wagner. Dr. Wagner, recently of Colorado Springs and faculty member at Fuller Theological Seminary and Vision

International University, has written a classic volume describing the growth of the church in Latin America. A brief review of his work will provide one vantage point of church growth, which I call the "Power Dynamic."

In Dr. Wagner's book, *Spiritual Power and Church Growth*, he presents convincing evidence of the power of God as a primary component of church growth. He focuses on the sovereign move of God as seen in Latin America, where the primary method of evangelism is through dynamic preaching and the manifested gifts of the Holy Spirit in action. The leadership in Latin America were/are active in taking the Gospel to the streets, causing tremendous results for the expansion of the church. Further, discipleship within the confines of the local church, and a focus on church planting, has been the prime motivation and activity of the Latin American revival.

Another perspective on church growth is presented by Carl F. George in his book, *How to Break Growth Barriers*. Mr. George's book fits a common genre of books advocating a change in management style to increase the numbers of a local church. Written for the Western market, he focuses on "an emphasis on leadership development... A systems-based, managerial approach, when prayerfully operated in dependence on the Holy Spirit, is the most effective way to deliver the most widespread continuing infusion of desperately needed care. It also models most closely the way Jesus worked with his twelve disciples" (see his text, page 15).

The search for a model of dynamic growth is always linked to the style of ministry of Christ. George and other writers believe leadership is the key to growth of the Church. He advocates a paradigm shift, from the "sheepherder" to a "rancher" mentality. He states; "You cannot deliver help to all people at the levels they require. Instead, you must take a more managerial, conceptual view of things, which in the long run is not only most loving but is the perspective Jesus exemplified" (pg. 19).

George maintains that the true leader must provide a way for the needs of the people to be met without attempting (in vain) to meet all the needs alone. Good advice, indeed, yet wisdom is always needed in regards to what burdens to bear and which are for someone else. A truly effective leader is able to accomplish goals through the efforts of others.

From George's perspective, the key to the whole process of church growth is an expanded vision. Truly, without vision the people perish (Prov. 29:18). Leaders with a large vision usually accomplish more than those with a limited vision. However, as will be discussed in detail later, having a large vision without the proper biblical perspective may accomplish great things, but may be wood, hay and stubble in the final analysis. It is essential to have a vision consistent with the clearly communicated Word of God, and in line with our level of gifting and authority.

Vision motivates people in a certain direction. A vision statement can galvanize a church to a specific call. When plans and purposes with accountability are added to the vision, it sets the stage for growth in a given direction.

Finally, George presents an important consideration regarding growth bias. If the mentality of a local church is that "Small is better," the possibility for growth is stilted. These biases must be confronted. The church must develop strategies for growth once the determination is made that growth is acceptable to the leaders.

A third view, espoused by Professor Donald McGavran in his book, Understanding Church Growth, encompasses the need for a foundation of theological understanding for church growth, integrating theology with an indigenous principle.

Specifically, Dr. McGavran speaks of faithfulness to God as the key to church growth. Faithfulness can be expressed by the constrained love of Christians, pressing forward to tell the Good News of Christ, showing faithfulness in finding the lost and restoring them to the fold of God's plan for the ages (pg. 5).

"Wholesome growth also means faithful obedience to God in developing churches so solid in their human matrix that they can grow..." (pg. 6). It is not merely a sociological or anthropological process. Basically, growth is theological in nature.

"God requires it. The Bible provides the direction for what God wants done. It believes that Acts 4:12, John 14:6 and scores of similar passages are true. It holds that belief in Jesus Christ, understood according to the scriptures, is necessary for salvation. Church growth rises in unshakable theological conviction" (pg. 7).

It is from Dr. McGavran's frame of reference that this book is written. Certainly there are natural or strategic patterns and programs that can be followed which may enhance church growth. However, if the theological mandate of growth and the patterns of the Word of God are not adequately followed, one may produce a facsimile of a church without producing "The Church" which would be in accordance with the will and purpose of God.

McGavran provides several reasons, from his extensive research, for growth, or the lack of growth. His listing and comments are most insightful. Some of the reasons for growth include:

1.) Some minister, layman or missionary dedicated his or her life to planting churches.

2.) That the Gospel was preached to a clearly receptive part of the Mosaic (Acts 2:13).

3.) That some church men recognized one of the many growing points given by God to His Church. He valued this beginning and poured his life into it.

4.) Someone had a particular plan for multiplying churches which fit a special population. He prayed for months and years that men and women would be won and churches multiplied. He then worked as planned.

5.) Environmental and church factors favorable to growth appeared at the same time. For example, in Korea in 1919 Christians led the freedom movement that made Christianity popular. At the same time, the Methodists launched a great forward movement.

6.) A Christian leader devised a broad pattern of action which multiplied congregations, such as Nevius in Shang Tung, China.

7.) Some church men/women refused to be tied to work which did not plant churches, or some Christian leader discovered the difference between good church work and the chief purpose of Christian missions, and turned from one to the other.

8.) The Christian religion became "our religion" to a sizable segment of some culture. Indigenous leaders out of the sub-culture being converted were put in charge of the church.

9.) Indigenous church principles, and people-movement principles, were used together in some prepared people.

10.) The church and mission have prolonged post-baptismal Christian training to Christians and their children and grandchildren. Herbert Money of Peru notes that in 1964, Peru had 1500 Evangelical missionaries. The Seventh Day Adventists had only 20.5% of the total. Nevertheless, they had more than half of the Evangelical church members in Peru. Money credits Adventist effectiveness to systematic baptismal indoctrination as a key to their growth.

11.) Able leaders in the church were converted and praying Christians, filled with the Holy Spirit. A revival came to the church. There are many examples of this now being presented in church growth conferences throughout North America.

McGavran then summarized reasons for the lack of growth. They include:

1.) Leaders were chained to existent maintenance work, or church and mission were devoted to a non-productive pattern once needed, but long since outmolded.

2.) Church and mission were devoted to an only slightly productive pattern, instead of a highly productive one. For example, they continued Sunday school programs which no longer reached children. In international settings, they baptized no illiterates, though this limited the church largely to youth. They required a three-year catechism, though few adults could complete the course. They tried to circumvent polygamy by baptizing chiefly unmarried youth, hoping they would stick to monogamy.

3.) They did not learn the language of the people. They communicated in English only and so established the image that the Christian religion signifies mainly cultural advantage. They influenced a few of the rebel young men on their way out of the tribe, but very few old men or families were subsequently won to Christ.

4.) Fearing the problems which are often the result of new Christians joining a church, they set very high standards for membership and baptized very few.

5.) The minister was perceived as too highly trained and was not "one" with the people. Further, because of too high an income need, the minister could not be supported by the local indigenous churches themselves. Church and mission allowed themselves to remain isolated in an area of low potential.

6.) They worked with resistant homogenous groups instead of baptizing the receptive ones who were available to them.

7.) Leaders did not learn about church growth from mistakes made in the past.

8.) Evaluation as to the effectiveness of evangelistic effort was lacking. In other words, little follow-up was done to determine the results of one's efforts.

9.) The mission, faced with little growth, did not seek expert opinion from the outside. This is often needed for true church growth to occur. It is necessary to have a set of eyes from outside of the organization who can objectivity provide needed guidance and wisdom to move a church or ministry from one place or one level to another.

10.) They accepted gradualism (slow growth over time) as a sufficient mission method, rather than looking for dynamic growth (Pages 162, 163 of McGavran's book).

Building bridges and bold planning are keys to church growth. Church growth requires the building of a relationship within a community context, which is multi-cultural and evangelistic in orientation. Bridges to others will not be realized as long as the church remains behind the safe walls of the worship center. Reaching out to the community through other secular organizations, schools, civic circles, etc., can be a way of building a relational bridge and touching the lives of members of the community.

Of course, one must have a goal of reaching the community (or the nations). McGavran lists three essential steps in setting appropriate goals to achieve the task.

They begin with an emphasis on evangelism as a thoroughly biblical mandate for all believers. The Church has been pastor focused, believing that it was the pastor's role to win the lost, while the congregation cheers on. This remains a stronghold of thinking in many evangelical and charismatic churches. The mandate of Ephesians 4:11-16 states;

> *And He Himself gave some to be apostles, some prophets, some evangelists, and some pastors and teachers,*
>
> *for the equipping of the saints for the work of ministry, for the edifying of the Body of Christ,*
>
> *till we all come to the unity of the faith and of the knowledge of the Son of God, to a perfect man, to the measure of the stature of the fullness of Christ;*
>
> *that we should no longer be children, tossed to and fro and carried about with every wind of doctrine, by the trickery of men, in the cunning craftiness of deceitful plotting,*
>
> *but, speaking the truth in love, may grow up in all things into Him who is the head; Christ;*
>
> *from whom the whole body, joined and knit together by what every joint supplies, according to the effective working by which every part does its share, causes growth of the body for the edifying of itself in love.*

It is the responsibility of those who are Christ's gifts to the Church (the five-fold ministry) to prepare the people of God to work in God's vineyard. The work of ministry (service) is to be carried on by an equipped, trained and restored laity, empowered by the Holy Spirit, who are actively functioning to reach the lost, discipling them to maturity.

The faults within the Church of the present are too numerous to list, but are a combination of the attitudes of the laity ("You keep them humble Lord, we'll keep them poor," "Pastors come and go," "If he performs to our liking we'll keep him," etc.) and the "professional" clergy community where the pastor is responsible for everything, unwilling to share responsibility and glory.

To win the world this paradigm must change.

A realistic picture of the past is necessary, which comes through the charting of past growth. The best predictor of present and future behavior is past behavior. Past behavior will continue in the present. This is always true unless an intervention occurs. Charting past growth can be a wake-up call to begin to search for answers and attempt new God-given strategies for future change.

One must also make faith projections, looking for growth through the eyes of vision and faith. These goals must be published, discussed, developed, communicated and followed by strategies to accomplish the goals given under the guidance of the Holy Spirit.

Whatever one's strategy for growth, biblical patterns, judiciously followed, will lead (in time) to biblical results.

The church in America, which is exported to the rest of the world, is often filled with the latest programs and plans which are rarely (apparently) compared to the Word, the plan and purpose of God. In this book the patterns found in the Word of God are explored from a theological basis, so the foundations of the Church can be strongly established, and the Kingdom of God expanded.

METHODS OF GROWING AND THE METHOD OF JESUS

The procedure Jesus followed to increase the Kingdom of God on this earth is frequently overlooked in modern church growth strategy. Jesus called two pair of fishermen and promised to make them fishers of men (Matthew 4:18-22). Before He called them, He prayed all night, seeking the wisdom of the Father, and then He hand-picked twelve men from among the disciples that were already following Him to become His apostles (Luke 6:12-13). When He called them, He called them primarily to come and be with Him. Because, as we will see in greater detail later, Jesus' focus of ministry was impartational of the Father's plans and purposes. He would train and teach His disciples to eventually be sent out with the Good News of the Kingdom of God.

"Jesus did not intend to spread the Gospel without the assistance of others. Jesus intended to bring people into the kingdom by means of the cooperative efforts of a community of believers."[1]

"Jesus had a definite plan in mind when He sent the twelve disciples out to win the world. He not only used them but He eventually gathered 70 others who were also instructed in all the things necessary for evangelism and discipleship. They were also commissioned and sent forward, two by two, to bring about the establishment of the Kingdom of God. It seems apparent that though Jesus did focus His attention on a selected few to impart the greater portion of His knowledge and wisdom to, yet His intention was to use the common man, the laity, who have been trained in proper leadership, to expand and establish the Kingdom of God. God's purpose for the growth of His Church is affirmed, not in some isolated passage of scripture, nor in one book or portion of a chapter, but in scripture in it's entirety. God's intent to save men is the witness of the whole Bible."[2]

The method Jesus used and demonstrated in His life and ministry was to <u>gather and scatter</u>.

First, Jesus assembled the apostles and gave them clear instructions concerning His plans and purposes. Undoubtedly, the disciples listened with great intentionality and observed the life of Christ most carefully. Jesus spent much of His time giving them instructions both publicly and privately while demonstrating for them through on-the-job training how to minister effectively to the needs of a lost and dying world.

Second, He sent them out under His supervision into towns and villages with a mission to preach and heal (Matthew 10:1).

---

[1] (Stokes, Mac - The Evangelism Of Jesus, Evangelistic Materials, Nashville, TN, 1968, pg. 79)
[2] (McGavran and Winfield, 10 Steps For Church Growth, Harper and Roe Publishers, New York, New York, 1977, pg. 35).

Jesus followed a method of gathering and going out.

He gathered the apostles for prayer and instruction, urging them to go out in missions of service and preaching. Over the generations, much of the methodology that Christ used has been lost in the development of congregational life, especially as seen in our modern-day Church.

But there is a wind of change on the horizon!

We have moved from the beginning of the Reformation under Martin Luther, from one type of congregation to another, with different forms of government and different mission strategies.

The Reformation, of course, has continued up until our present time. God has been restoring back to His Church the gifts found within the Word of God, including the five-fold ministry gifts of pastor, evangelist, teacher, prophet and apostle. Again, referring back to the work of C. Peter Wagner, there appears to be a new move of God that promises a return to early Church biblical patterns. Peter coined the phrase, "The New Apostolic Reformation," as a way to describe a networking of ministers and ministries in the Body of Christ around the world.

THE NEW APOSTOLIC REFORMATION[3]

"Rapidly increasing numbers of Christians in virtually every part of the world are finding themselves 'doing church' in ways distinctly different from the patterns of the past. If I (Dr. Wagner) am not mistaken, we are currently witnessing the most radical change in church life and structure since the Protestant Reformation of the 16th Century.

"I call this new movement 'The New Apostolic Reformation.' Some of us have also used the term 'post-denominationalism,' but the fact of the matter is that a significant number of the New Apostolic Churches are found right inside denominations such as the Southern Baptist

---

[3] Lecture, Dr. C. Peter Wagner for San Diego City Church Ministries, presented in October 1997 at Skyline Wesleyan Church.

Convention, the Evangelical Lutheran Church of America, the United Methodist Church and many others.

"The majority of them, however, have developed outside of the traditional structures.

"New Apostolic Churches have taken on a wide variety of forms. They range from huge metropolitan meta-churches and mega-churches to house churches in China, from churches of the rich to churches of the poor, from African independent churches to Latin American grassroots churches."

A few examples here in Southern California would be Anaheim Vineyard, Saddleback Community Church, The Church on the Way, and Crenshaw Christian Center.

The adjective "apostolic" carries two major connotations.

George G. Hunter III, of Asbury Seminary, discusses the first connotation of "apostolic" by writing that a major difference between apostolic congregations and traditional ones is that the apostolic congregations "...are reaching significant numbers of the unchurched, non-Christian, secular people in America's mission fields."

His new book, *Church for the Unchurched* (Abingdon Press) probes this in depth, saying, "traditional churches have much to learn from these pioneering churches."

A second connotation of "apostle" has to do with leadership authority. Large numbers of these churches agree that the biblical gift of the apostle and the office of the apostle are functioning in the Church today, just as in the first century.

Pastor David Cannistraci of Evangel Christian Fellowship has completed a textbook on that subject, published by Regal Books. Rather than organize themselves into denominations, these churches form "apostolic networks" which are clusters of free-standing churches that voluntarily submit to the authority of a leader recognized as an apostle. Some clusters do not use the word "apostle," but the function is the same.

Lyle Schaller, in his book, *The New Reformation* (Abingdon Press) likens these churches to the "new wineskins" spoken of by Jesus. He raises the provocative question: "Should the old wineskins be cleansed and patched to carry the Gospel of Jesus Christ to new generations in a new social context? Or should the investment of time, commitment and energy be made in new wineskins?"

It is in keeping with the concept of a New Apostolic Reformation that this book is written. There is no question that there is a need for new wineskins for the new wine of the Holy Spirit that is being poured out upon the nations of the world today. However, one must be careful not to toss out the baby with the bath water. It is quite true that there are biblical patterns which, when judiciously applied, can steer one's direction towards wise church development and growth. But to throw out the lessons learned from 2000 years of Church history would show a lack of wisdom and maturity.

Nonetheless, it is vital that the Church facing the 21st Century become prepared for radical and necessary changes to ready for the fully anticipated influx of souls which will come into the Kingdom as we approach the end of our age. To do so, we must understand the Church as God intended from the beginning, and focus on returning it to a place of normalcy, or to its intended purpose as found within the Word of God.

Perhaps a few of Dr. Wagner's powerful points can establish a foundation for the future. Dr. Wagner outlines 10 characteristics of the New Apostolic Churches. These include:

- They will have a <u>new name</u> — an Apostolic church, which defines its overall purpose and function.

- These churches will have a significant <u>new authority</u> delegated by the Holy Spirit to individuals rather than to church boards. This will cause a moving of these churches from a legal structure to primarily, a biblical one. Their main focus will be the implementation of

God's intended plan for the community. We will also see a change from a rational leadership style to that of a more charismatic leadership style. Not charismatic in terms of what we commonly call the gifts of the Holy Spirit, but charismatic in the sense that leaders who, through strong personalities, will bring about the fulfillment of God's purposes. The pastor is the leader in these New Apostolic Churches, rather than becoming an employee or "a hireling." Thus, the pastor's accountability in the local church has changed. They are becoming more like leaders rather than followers of the congregational life.

- A <u>new structure</u> is being developed which includes organizational structure, where the people are doing the ministry rather than the pastors. The people have given up leading and allowed the pastors to lead, whereas the pastors have given up ministry and allowed the people to minister. The leader's job is to equip the people for service. Much of the staff in these New Apostolic Churches is home grown. They have been trained as spiritual sons and daughters within the ministry. Many of them, in order to train effective leadership, are establishing their own Bible College programs within the local church structure. Thus, the leaders are being trained in a new and significant way.
- There is a <u>new focus</u>. Traditionally, churches have been generally driven by the pastor and their own church heritage. But in New Apostolic Churches, they are driven primarily by vision and secondarily by purpose.
- In New Apostolic Churches, there is a <u>new worship</u> style. A major element in the development of unity is worship, which is highly participatory, using various instruments and much creativity, including dancing and kneeling, lifting hands and extended times of worship, singing and rejoicing.

- A <u>new type of prayer</u>. Patterns are being established, including what is being called concert prayer, where entire congregations spontaneously pray together for a certain thing, perhaps led by the worship leader or the pastor.
- A <u>new financing</u>. In most of the New Apostolic Churches, there are relatively few financial problems, which is the result of strong teachings on the Christian's responsibility to bring tithes and offerings into the storehouse. This provides greater resources for the specific vision and mission of that local church.
- The word "apostolic" means "to reach the lost, sent out, church planting, church mission and social service." This is a part of <u>their new outreach</u>. Local church, directed and involved in outreach, means the pastor will often take teams into the Jerusalem, the Judea and the Samaria, or even to the uttermost parts of the Earth, from their own local church.
- There are <u>new power paradigms</u> found within the New Apostolic Churches. Spiritual authority has become most important, and the concept of headship is vital. Spiritual fatherhood, or mentoring, has become a very important part of these New Apostolic Churches. Also, the development of apostolic company and councils for mutual accountability based upon relationship are part of the New Apostolic Churches.
- The <u>home cell group</u> has become part of the major foundation for the vast majority of these New Apostolic Churches.

There are some new and wonderful things happening in the Kingdom of God!

At the same time, many dubious and problematic procedures detrimental to church growth remain in effect. Throughout the rest of this volume, comment will be made specifically about many of the issues raised by Dr. Wagner. It is my hope that as we deal with them, and look at the fundamental structures of church growth from a biblical perspective, we will discover the patterns necessary for building a healthy and vibrant Church to carry us strongly into the 21st Century.

As we will see, it will not be the denomination, nor the fully independent church that will lead in the next generation, but the interdependent gathering of God's ordained congregations worshipping together in the city for God's greater purposes.

But first, let us look back before we look forward.

END OF CHAPTER QUESTIONS

CHAPTER ONE

1. Are most churches in your city divided? How do we "build bridges" to build the church of the locality?
2. Where in the world is most growth in the Church happening today? Why?
3. List some keys to church growth.
4. What is a modern apostle? Can you name some?
5. How can a leader more clearly and quickly identify possible avenues of outreach and growth in a community?
6. What can the church in America learn from the move of God in Two-Thirds World nations?
7. How does the Church become more inclusive, remaining "free in the Spirit" but "tempered with discretion?"

Chapter Two

The Church From The Start

The Church is one of the most unlikely institutions God could choose to bring about His revelation. It's amazing to me as I think about the local church and the Church universal.

I was raised in an Evangelical Methodist church, a holiness denomination where, "You don't smoke or chew or go with girls who do." It was a church strong on personal salvation, being baptized, and a correct emphasis on learning God's Word about life and applying it to the best of one's ability. This church provided a wonderfully solid foundation, though it had many glowing weaknesses.

Of course, most churches do. I have yet to find a local church that does not have unique quirks about it (Perhaps you have noticed that as well). In spite of the many difficulties and inconsistencies of church life, the Church is God's chosen vehicle, and has been from the very beginning (see Eph. 1).

God's plan for the development of the Church must be set on a proper foundation to perpetuate God's Kingdom. In the present day, there are many governmental structures and differing styles of churches. Some are very formal or traditional, some very informal. Some seem to be accomplishing tremendous things for God and yet, upon closer examination of their internal structure, lack certain qualities of New Testament commitment. Other churches, seemingly small and insignificant, are positively impacting their community for Jesus Christ.

It's difficult to evaluate a church through observation alone.

In my spiritual walk I have wondered whether or not God had a different plan.

Isn't there a better way for us to reach the world for Christ than through the local church?

Could there eventually emerge a healthier place or more dynamic institution for the propagation of the Gospel, for instruction of the saints, for the development of a supportive community?

If not, why is the Church the way it is today?

If our modern version of church life is the way the Church is supposed to be, if this is God's plan from the beginning, why is it not more effective than what we are presently seeing?

There are many problems within local churches and the Body of Christ in general.

Perspective

The church in America has just traversed one of the most traumatic stages of its history, suffering through the fall of major ministry scandals, some for moral failure and financial improprieties, some due to burnout. When we take a hard and honest look at the Church, one can easily be discouraged at her as an institution. Yet, without question, God's perfect instrument for raising up young men and women to fulfill their destiny in God is the Church!

If there is a failure, it's not with God...it never is.

It certainly isn't with His Word...it never can be.

Therefore, the failure would have to be with what we have done with or to the Church through our misapplication of Bible principles. Perhaps through the ages we have taken what we believe the Bible says about the Church and twisted it in ways God never intended. What was God's original intention?

Should one find God's design, and if it were applied to the present in Twentieth Century Western Culture, what would the results be?

Beyond that, how can we as individual believers and as a community of faith be more actively involved in fulfilling what God would have us do in our present time?

To discover these theological keys could be life and ministry transforming.

A Biblical Framework

To fully understand God's intention, we must have a full biblical framework for church growth and development.

The Apostle Paul in I Corinthians 3 describes himself as an expert builder. As a builder, he laid down a full foundation based upon the revelation of Jesus Christ and the Gospel that He presented. It was Paul's hope that other builders would come after him and not rebuild the foundation, but build upon it for the strengthening and development of the Church. Without sound strategies and mission operations, which are based upon a firm theological foundation, we cannot see the fulfillment of God's purposes for building the church ("Cities: Missions/New Frontiers," Roger Greenway, pg. 81)[4].

To build a church, one must fully understand what should be the end result of that church. And although there can be great flexibility in terms of overall structure, there are certain characteristics of a truly New Testament church that must be a part of what is built in our modern society. These principles, which must be applied with flexibility and contextualized to modern culture, can be the foundation for seeing the Church become everything that God intended.

---

[4] To determine our Biblical foundation, it is necessary to begin in the beginning, with a clear review of patterns found in the Old Testament.

End of Chapter Questions

Chapter Two

1. How can leaders be instruments of change toward a more godly church?
2. Is God using your church in the manner in which He intended? Explain your response.
3. How can the Church be more effective in meeting needs and reaching the lost?
4. What was/is God's original intention for the Church? How close or far, in your opinion, are we from fulfilling God's intention?

Chapter Three

One Under God

Throughout Old Testament scriptures, God's servants were told to work according to patterns provided by God. Adam was to name the animals (Gen. 2:19), Noah to build the ark (Gen. 6:3), Moses to build the tabernacle in the wilderness according to the heavenly pattern (Ex. 26:1), David instructed his son, Solomon to follow the architectural and operational plan for the building of the temple (I Chron. 28:11). In each case, when they followed the pattern, the glory of God was manifested and God's purposes were fulfilled.

Much of church growth methodologies follow patterns, but often lack the blueprint of God. The scripture presents patterns for worship and patterns for prayer. Most germane to our study, patterns can be found, beginning in the Old Testament, for building God's Kingdom on Earth.

Before the Beginning

According to the Word of God, from the very beginning of time, God had the Church in mind (Eph 1). God has always intended for the Church to exist, but the fullness of the plan of God was not revealed until Christ came.

The Church didn't begin at Pentecost; it began in the beginning, before anything else existed. It began in the mind and intention of God! It was not an afterthought. Some have suggested that God merely adapted. Since Judaism was not working, God decided to shift His efforts to the Greeks and the Romans.

Of course, this was not the case.

God in His perfect foreknowledge knew everything that would ever occur. He knew in advance the progress of history. He knew in advance what He intended for His

Church. So, we must begin our study, not from Pentecost, but from the very beginning.

A Right Perspective

As Westerners, we think from a very individualistic viewpoint. Western nations are strong on individual rights. When the Western church discusses salvation, we talk about individual salvation. "I am born-again, I am Spirit filled." This is not the focus of other cultures; they do not think in similar fashion. They would never consider salvation merely as an individual experience, separated from community. True salvation includes families, cities and nations.

The Western mind interprets creation from an individualistic position. That is, God created man and woman, placed them in the garden, with their lives being separate from community. God was not just creating individuals, He was creating community. Remember, from the beginning it says, *"... It was not good for mankind to be alone, I will make a helpmate suitable," (Gen. 2:18).*

This refers to marriage — for the purpose of family. The man and the woman in the Garden of Eden had an innate understanding of this truth. They knew children would be part of their relationship. They had seen the model of the animal kingdom, with expectation of their own future.

God's purpose was to create community! This community was to espouse equality as a prime virtue before God. They were a community of covenant keepers, in relationship with God and with one another, with a common purpose.

What purpose did God give man in Genesis 1?

That we would rule and reign, subdue or control the whole earth! This was to be accomplished jointly, husband-wife, man-woman. God created the family, which is the foundation of communal life, as the beginning point for all His purposes.

Everything changed because of the fall. That is, everything but God's original intention. He created man and woman for the purpose of community, and for life on Earth that would bring glory to Him. Through family communities, He would establish His Kingdom on Earth.

The importance of community can be observed in Noah's life. It was Noah — and his family — saved by the Ark! The purpose was to again create a godly community. When God called Abraham "the great man of faith," He didn't just call Abraham or Abraham and Sarah. He brought the whole Klan with him. It was a community of faith that God desired to establish, co-laborers and inheritors of His world with the Lord.

Another Genesis story illustrates the importance of community. When Cain slew his brother Abel, and God confronted him, Cain replied, "What am I, my brothers keeper?" God never responded to the question because it did not need or deserve a response. Of course, we are our brothers' keepers, because we are community!

Westerners have focused too much on individualism. Even in churches, the whole focus of life is, "I want to go to a Bible study so that I will learn." "I want to experience a blessing so that I will grow, so I can be perfect and better than anyone else." In society, nobody wants to be on the bottom, everybody wants to be on the top. Everyone desires to be the most spiritual, the best liked, the most loved, the most wanted. We even interpret scripture according to incessant personal application — a morbid pre-occupation with self. Some would have it "Just Jesus and me." God never intended it to be "Jesus and me." It was "Jesus and we" — Community.

The Hebrew Perspective

From a Hebrew viewpoint, all life is spiritual.

From an Eastern perspective, all life has meaning.

Thus, we are all responsible to a greater community: the community of faith that God desires to build. Inherent in humanity, as seen through studies in cultural anthropology and sociology, is the need to gather together as people.

Even in America there is a need to affiliate. People want to join the best ministerial fellowship, seek to become part of the best denominational group, the "in" church or Rotary (versus Kiwanis), etc. We join to gain a sense of belonging and meaning. We join in an attempt to satisfy a universal need, inherent within us, to gather, to be apart of something. John Donne once wrote, "No man is an island." Except Donne tried to be an island. History tells us that he was a very lonely, bitter man, eventually committing suicide (the ultimate self-centered act). He tried to live life on his own terms, becoming an emotional isolate, an island unto himself, which led him to absolute despair.

God created mankind with a need for community. He gathers those who believe for fellowship. Even at the tower of Babel, rebellious men gathered with the hope of reaching God. The Bible says, *"If they are able to do this, nothing will stand in their way" (Gen. 11:1-9).* The principle and power of agreement is so strong that nothing can stand in the way of mankind's fulfillment. Through the life of the patriarchs to the time of Moses, several wonderful things happened. God's power was demonstrated, His grace manifested, His plan established.

Not just to individuals, but to communities.

Moses as Model

It was not for Moses' sake that God made him leader over Israel. It was necessary to have a leader to bring about the deliverance of the children of Israel. They were a community that had suffered under slavery and bondage, and needed to be set free. Moses was set in place for a divine purpose.

The Exodus under Moses provides an Old Testament picture of the Church. The children of Israel in the wilderness were a community that had been desperately broken due to slavery under Pharaoh. In like fashion, Christ came to deliver all mankind, lost and hopeless, under slavery to sin. Christ came, not just for a certain ethnic group or socio-economic class. He is the deliverer of all mankind from bondage, darkness and sin.

Mankind needed a Savior. Moses became a savior to bring about the deliverance of the people of God. Not only for the purpose of setting them free, but so that they would be gathered together.

For what?

For a purpose that God had designed from the beginning of time — to become the church in the wilderness.

Moses brought God's people out with a grand purpose or vision, to bring them into a land of promise. Abraham's covenant was established through Moses who delivered the law, necessary to understand sin and our responsibility to one another and God. Through Joshua, the possession of Israel's inheritance, or coming into the fullness of God's plan and purpose, occurred. In David, we see triumph over the tyrannical, the rejoicing and prosperity that God intends. The fulfillment of the Old Testament Church and the establishment of the Kingdom of God unfolds under David and Solomon's rule.

In Hebrew tradition, a detailed account of all of God's dealings with His people was kept, first orally, then in writing. The events of history were initially memorized, transmitted by the parents and elders, eventually becoming written so God's people would understand and obey His principles.

In Deuteronomy (see chapter 6), the responsibility for the fathers and mothers of the faith to train, teach and transmit godly principles to children is emphasized. From the time children were very young, they were taught all the historical stories, the meaning of the Passover, the laws of God, etc. — all things necessary to ingrain into the children a sense of God's plan and purpose for their lives.

Parents transmitted values, purpose and vision for their future. They understood God's precepts according to what their parents told them (assuming they did their job properly). Thus, if they followed the precepts of God, if they behaved according to God's plan, they would prosper, be blessed and come into the fulfillment of God's plan for their lives. If they failed to do so, God would remove His blessing, which would open the door for curses that would come upon them (See Deut. 27- 28).

God's plan was to transmit these principles through family and through community over time. None of it occurred instantaneously. It took time, commitment to community, and a plan to insure God would be glorified, and family integrity would be maintained.

Many people believe and teach that if you have had one year of Bible school, you should know it all. You should be filled with the knowledge, purpose and plan of God, and be able to leap tall buildings in a single bound.

It just doesn't work that way.

Maturity in character and knowledge of the things of God is something that comes to us line-upon-line and precept-upon-precept. It takes time to see the fulfillment of God's life in our own.

This principle was clearly understood from an Old Testament viewpoint. The nation of Israel knew their prime responsibility was to start training children when they were mere babies, telling them stories of faith and demonstrating what it means to be a member of a community of faith. The entire focus of the Hebrew viewpoint of covenant relationship with God was _we_, not me. They were much more concerned about the way a child behaved in public, not because of the negative reflection on them as parents, but because of the negative reflection on the whole community. It wasn't just, "I feel ashamed because my child did something wrong." They were conscious of their responsibility to the entire community. All of the community of believers had an equal sense of responsibility for everybody else in that community.

Their attitude parallels the attitude in the forties and fifties in America. If a child did something at another person's house that was inappropriate, and the parent of the house caught that child, they corrected the child, maybe even spanked him/her. The non-parent would then take the child by the hand to his/her home. When that child arrived home, the parent would thank the non-parent for correcting the child. They would thank them for bringing the child home and apologize for their child's misbehavior. Further discipline was likely to follow. Parents were grateful for assistance and support in the parenting process. Since parents cannot be at all places at the same time, the community help was seen as a blessing.

This is not the view today!!!

Individual rights and political correctness are the bywords of modern culture. The parent today frequently becomes hostile and resentful if someone else "dares" to correct "my child." This individualism is one of many reasons for the terrible deterioration in society of basic community.

Truly there is a limited sense of community in Western culture, with few exceptions.

One exception should be the Church. The Church, designed by the Lord from the beginning, is to be a place of community. We have strayed so very far from God's intention.

This Sunday

This Sunday, in virtually every Western Culture, an interesting phenomenon will occur. Men, women and their children, those who have given their hearts and lives to the Lord Jesus Christ, will dress in the appropriate attire required for their local fellowship, hopefully remember to gather up their Bibles, pile into their vehicle and drive whatever distance necessary to reach their local church. When they arrive, hopefully not in too frazzled a condition, they will enter the doors of a building that has been set aside for the purpose of worship. It is called the church. Of course, we all know it is not a church, but merely a building. It is the people that are the church. They will enter into the doors, hopefully in somewhat of a positive mindset, seeing people that they most likely have not communicated with for at least a week, perhaps longer. They will sit, usually in isolation from others, perhaps finding one or two people with whom they know and enjoy a connection. Most likely, these are the same people they connected with the week prior. They will sing some songs, give an offering, hear announcements, receive (hopefully) an inspiring message of encouragement, and leave virtually unchanged from when they entered the doors of the building.

Certainly, this is an abnormal or at least sub-normal description of the Church Christ came to establish.

There must be something more than just "Sunday, go to meeting" in church, or even Sunday morning, Sunday night, Wednesday night. Certainly, Christ came to establish something more powerful than a place to go to remove a sense of loneliness for a moment.

This is a totally sub-normal expression of the Church of Jesus Christ!

The Church in the Bible is a vibrant fellowship of men and women who were far from perfect, but who had established within their own hearts a desire to become part of a community where there was mutual accountability and responsibility to one another. Where daily fellowship, prayer, apostolic instruction and the breaking of bread was the lifeblood of their very existence.

We have strayed far from God's original intention. But, perhaps as we look through the Bible again, reviewing Old and New Testament patterns of gathering, we will be able to ascertain God's intention for the Church of the 21st Century.

End of Chapter Questions

Chapter Three

1. Can we attribute the profusion of groups such as "Pro-Choice" and the "Gay and Lesbian Coalition" to the degradation of our sense of community? Explain your thoughts.
2. If God's initial intention was to create communities, not just save individuals, does the man or woman who sees or hears the Word as only pertaining to him/herself really know what community means? Explain.
3. Is intercessory prayer a way of taking responsibility for each other? If so, how? If not, why not?
4. How, in this "Me Generation," could you instill the knowledge of being your "brother's keeper"?
5. What are some of the differences in Western (American individuals) thinking and other culture's (community) thinking?
6. What are some of the patterns God gave in the Bible for church growth?
7. What was God's original intent for creating man and woman?
8. As a nation, how do we return to the early American/godly tradition of raising our children in a community and not merely as separate individuals?
9. What tools can we use to inspire a sense of community responsibility when the world's message is so consuming with individual pursuit?

Chapter Four

According To Patterns

The teachings of the Old Testament began with oral tradition. That is, they began with the telling of stories describing what occurred in the lives and times of the children of Israel. These stories were passed down from generation to generation. Eventually, these oral traditions were compiled by various scribes and put into written form under the authority of the prophets and priests within Israel. The keeping, transcribing and teaching of the scripture was seen as a highly sacred trust. Thus, one of the highest callings (after that of a parent) in the Old Testament was a priest, scribe or prophet. All three were actively involved in the transmission of God's progressive revelation to the community of faith.

Probably the best model for those ministries can be seen in the life of Ezra, a scribe and priest who eventually became a judge in Israel. He was one of the most effective teachers of God's Word, transmitting God's truth to His people. In the book of Ezra, chapter 7, verse 10, one can see some of the keys to his success in terms of ministry. Further, one can see the importance God gave to the teaching of His Word through the life and ministry of this great Old Testament man of God.

Beginning in Ezra, chapter 7, verse 6, we read,

"This Ezra went up from Babylon and he was a scribe skilled in the law of Moses which the Lord God of Israel had given. And the king granted him all that he requested because the hand of the Lord his God was upon him."

Then, in verse 9-10 it continues,

"For on the first of the first month he began to go up from Babylon and on the first of the fifth

month he came to Jerusalem, because the good hand of his God was upon him. For Ezra had set his heart to study the law of the Lord and to practice it and to teach his statutes and ordinances in Israel." (NAS)

Ezra was in captivity when he first determined in his heart to prepare himself for greater service. As a member of the community of faith, being one who was chosen by birth for the priesthood, he understood his awesome responsibility not just before God, or merely to himself, or even to his family, but to the whole community of faith found in Babylon, and ultimately to be reestablished in Israel. His responsibility was to apply himself to become the best at whatever God would have for him to be. He owed it to his community. To do less would be a shameful waste of the talent that God had placed in him.

In terms of Ezra's training, he was first a scribe, tasked to transfer scripture from page to page, and writing the words for a prophet or priest. Everything transmitted had to be done with absolute perfection. If in the transmission from one page to another, one error was made, the entire page had to be destroyed and the project begun again. Thus, scribes learned to be careful in their work. After all, the Scriptures were sacred; holy, the Words of God. Ezra was a highly skilled scribe who paid close attention to every detail in his work.

The Bible indicates that Ezra eventually became a judge. This powerful governmental position presents a progression in his ministry responsibilities. Yet, from a natural perspective, one cannot find anything specifically special about him. One thing can be seen for certain — God's good hand was upon him.

Some brief comments on Ezra as a type may be helpful. As members of the Body of Christ, God's good hand is already upon each of us. In fact, His Spirit lives within us. One cannot get much better than that. Yet, the sense of responsibility to do, function and fulfill a destiny does not seem to motivate most people in the Body of Christ today. Perhaps because of a lack of proper understanding of the Scripture, since our understanding is filtered through a Western mindset, rather than an Eastern worldview.

The Western mindset evolves from Greek philosophy, which is dualistic in orientation. That is, the world is viewed as secular and sacred, and the two rarely meet. In modern vernacular, one would act differently at the "work-world" outside of the "church-world," since the "work-world" is secular. Thus, there are secular rules that apply to life in a secular setting, according to Greek tradition. For instance, in the business world, if a person is going to be successful, he/she must "swim with the sharks." There are certain principles, if applied, which will assist the businessman towards a successful venture. Unfortunately, many of these rules are often highly suspect at best and blatantly not biblical at worst.

From a Hebraic viewpoint, this worldview makes limited sense. From their viewpoint, business is spiritual. Thus, one's ethics should follow God's Word. In modern day, having a Greek mentality, many Christians will proclaim, "When I come to church, or if I am in a Bible study, then I will be highly spiritual. I will worship, I may even dance, and I will certainly wear the correct clothing. I will demonstrate to everyone how spiritual I am."

These actions and attitudes are accepted in the Christian community. "I do what is expected to be a spiritual man or woman." It is often the way people are socialized into church life. If people accept this socialization as the norm, and they enter the "real world" with a mask to survive in that social setting, it will cause them to lose their salt-and-light influence in the world.

Image was not a major concern for the Hebrews, since all life was seen as spiritual. They asked, "What does God want in this situation?" The closest one can come in the present day to that thought pattern is, "What would mom say if I did something?", or "What would my dad say if he was looking over my shoulder?"

Unfortunately, in modern society, one rarely sees the sense of healthy shame that needs to be exhibited when something is done wrong. This shows a blatant lack of understanding of commitment as members of a community.

The decisions Ezra made and the effects of those decisions were important. We see that he "set his heart" (vs. 10). The word "set" means "to firmly establish without intention, to move from the place that one has set themselves." Of course, he did not set his intentions on just anything. He set his heart, the center of his being to study the law so he might understand it, making application of the law to his life and preparing himself to communicate it effectively in the future.

Then it says, "To practice it," which has a dual meaning. On one hand, it speaks about the importance of making personal applications of the Word of God so He might change the heart and mind of a person. It speaks of the transformation of an individual's character; a most important result (hopefully) of the study of God's Word.

It also means to practice the ministry or the gifting of God as provided by the Lord to that individual. Thus, from the time Ezra was a young man in the community of faith, he practiced the ministry to which he was called. Long before he became a skilled scribe, he was a student, preparing his heart and mind for servanthood. Long before he ever taught the Word of God, he would practice his teaching through his dialogue with his fellow students and in ministry, as God gave him an open door.

Ezra is one of many examples of men (women) used by God for the transmission of God's plans and patterns in the Church of the Old Testament. Men and women, many with significant personal character flaws and inconsistencies in life, were called of God, trained and taught from childhood to set their hearts to the highest calling, the transmission of God's Word. When Israel followed the pattern of obedience to the Word of God, following His purposes as described (often by the prophets), God's blessing or special favor came upon His people. When they forgot their covenant with God and their covenant with their fellow members within the community, the results were captivity and domination. As King David stated, *"One generation shall praise Thy works to another, and shall declare Thy mighty acts,"* (Psalm 145:4).

God's purpose was to continue to bless His people from generation to generation as they followed the patterns of training their children and young people to serve the Lord with gladness of heart.

God's plan, revealed in the history of His covenant with Abraham (Gen. 15), was for all nations to be blessed by Israel. This covenant was initially actualized through Moses, expanded in David and Solomon, but was not fully revealed until Christ, when the door to the Kingdom came in fulfillment of the promise.

Long before Christ came, it was prophesied that His Kingdom would be inclusive (all nations), multi-cultural (all peoples), both spiritual and natural. Many of the scriptures following will help establish His purpose as we discover the patterns of God from the Old Testament and then later in the New.

GOVERNMENT UNDER GOD

Isaiah, more than any other prophet, speaks of the future Kingdom and the Messiah to come. In Isaiah 53, He is described as the suffering servant, the lamb slain from the foundation of the world. However, it is in Isaiah 9:6-7 that the primary purposes of the Messiah are presented.

> *"For a Child will be born to us, a Son will be given to us and the government will rest on His shoulders. And His name will be called wonderful counselor, Mighty God, Eternal Father, Prince of Peace. There will be no end to the increase of His government or of peace on the throne of David and over His Kingdom to establish it and to uphold it*

with justice and righteousness. From then on and forever more, the zeal of the Lord of Hosts will accomplish this."

In Isaiah 11:1-6, 9b, the method for the empowerment of the Kingdom is established.

> "And the Spirit of the LORD will rest on Him, The spirit of wisdom and understanding, The spirit of counsel and strength, The spirit of knowledge and the fear of the LORD. And He will delight in the fear of the LORD, And He will not judge by what His eyes see, Nor make a decision by what His ears hear; But with righteousness He will judge the poor, And decide with fairness for the afflicted of the earth; And He will strike the earth with the rod of His mouth, And with the breath of His lips He will slay the wicked. Also righteousness will be the belt about His loins, And faithfulness the belt about His waist. And the wolf will dwell with the lamb, And the leopard will lie down with the kid, And the calf and the young lion and the fatling together; And a little boy will lead them... For the earth will be full of the knowledge of the LORD As the waters cover the sea."

There is so much that could be presented from these passages, but a few brief comments will have to suffice.

The identity of the Messiah would be manifested as Wonderful Counselor, Mighty God, Everlasting Father, Prince of Peace. Jesus was all of these and more. His rule would never end, and the government would be on His shoulders; He would have the authority to rule over all.

Of course, Christ has been proclaimed forever King of Kings and Lord of lords. Yet the Church, which grasped in the beginning the significance of Christ's transference of authority to His Apostles (Matthew 28:18-20), seems to have forgotten Christ's everlasting rule, and His intention since John the Baptist to establish His government through His Church on the earth.

This rule would be inclusive, encompassing the powerful and powerless, the rich and poor, the strong and weak (Isaiah 9:5). Further, He would rule with justice and mercy, giving power to the powerless, and providing humility to those who sensed they had power. All of this would be accomplished through the zeal of the Lord, which is ultimately the outpouring of the Holy Spirit, prophesied throughout the Old Testament, fulfilled initially in the book of Acts and continuing to be fulfilled in our present day.

Christ is the Head of the Church!

We, His body. The shoulders are a part of the Body, which receives its authority from the head.

The power to accomplish this rule is thoroughly divine, supernatural. This power is the fullness of the Spirit of God (counsel, might), which was embodied in Christ and poured out on the covenant community at Pentecost (Acts 1:8; 2:1-4). The purpose was and is the establishment of the Church, which the gates of hell cannot stop (Matthew 16:18) from progressing until all things are complete and presented to Christ for His glory, and then to the Father.

This was, and still is, God's plan.

His messenger was Christ, the message, the Gospel, the mandate passed on to His Apostles unto the present. However, Jesus accomplished His mission through transference of His life to His chosen ones. He provided the pattern, which when empowered by the Holy Spirit, will bring the same or similar results as seen in the First Century Church. The discovery of the pattern is one of the prime purposes of this generation.

Fulfilling the pattern is the task of the Church.

THE TEMPLE

The focus of Hebrew life, beginning in the time of Solomon, became temple worship. A deep desire for God's people to attend temple worship as often as possible was evident. All of God's people were required to attend temple worship. If one was in a far, distant land, then they could attend annually, making a pilgrimage to Jerusalem to worship in this holy place.

All of temple life is so wonderfully symbolic of what worship can be. There are many types, shadows and patterns useful for today presented in temple life. To worship God freely was the highest desire. Even though the children of Israel were not under grace, but the law, there was a sense of wonder about God's purposes for life as they participated in temple worship.

The Jews, in general, had a zest for living that would make most Christians embarrassed and humbled in comparison. The Jewish believers understood that God chose them. Though they were at one time an insignificant people, God by His power made them a great nation, bringing them into a marvelous inheritance; thus, the least they could do was to give God His due...to give Him sacrifice, praise and worship.

THE COMMUNITY GROWS

As the community of faith began to grow and the world began to change, centralized places of worship separate from the temple were established known as synagogues. The synagogue began in captivity as a gathering place designed to be a miniature of the temple. It was a place of instruction, a community center, a place of great activity for many parts of social life, including weddings. The synagogue was the center of all activities for an outlying community that could not attend temple worship on a regular basis. It was in synagogues and through rabbis that God's purpose was transmitted, generation after generation, to the time of Christ. As we will see later, Christ's ministry was that of a rabbi. He was a teacher, sent from God.

Beginning in the garden and acted out in stages, God adding revelation over time to the children of Israel, prepared mankind for the time of Christ. Prior to the arrival of Jesus, Israel had been in nearly 400 years of occupation by various governments. At the time of Christ, they were under the occupation of the Roman Empire. There had not been a prophetic voice of any significance for these 400 years.

The people of God, in captivity in Judaea, were in a position to hear something from God because they had continued in their religious tradition. Though Herod the Great had re-built the temple for worship, it was not the same as it was under the glory and grandeur of the administration of David and Solomon. Israel was an occupied territory. Thus, they had to share the glory of God and the glory of their history with this uncircumcised Roman hoard.

When Christ came, it was a time of great anticipation! People would commonly cry out, "Would this not be a good time for the Messiah to come?" They were looking for a deliverer. A Moses. They were hoping for a Gideon or a Deborah. They were longing for someone who would bring liberation to them. Jesus came to a community fragmented because of the apostasy of the religious leaders of the day. The Israelites were the hungry and thirsty, longing to be filled.

The people of God were in a position to receive because they were broken and fragmented. That which they needed, of course, was and is Christ. But they did not understand who Jesus was, nor what He came to do. There were certain aspects of His ministry that were familiar and necessary for them to establish a sense of faith in what He was saying and doing.

"But when the time had fully come, God sent His Son born of a woman, born under the law." (Gal. 4:4)

POLITICAL CONTRIBUTIONS

There were certain political circumstances that led to the perfect timing of Christ, especially through the handiwork of the Romans. The Romans, as no other people up until their day, developed a belief in the unity of mankind under universal law. Under Roman occupation, there was a freedom of movement about the Mediterranean world that would have been most difficult for the messengers of the Gospel before the reign of Augustus Caesar (From 27 B.C. to A.D. 14).

The Roman road system provided easy passageways that had not previously existed. Palestine, where Judaea and Israel are today, was the central travel route between Europe, Africa and Asia. It was and still is a most strategic area linking the Old World together. Judea became the central stage for all commerce and business in the Old World.

The role of the Roman army in the development of the ideal of universal organization and the spread of the Gospel should not be ignored. The introduction of Christianity to the British Isles was a result of the efforts of Christian soldiers stationed there. The conquest of the Romans led to a loss of belief by many peoples in their gods, because the gods had not been able to keep them from the defeat of the Romans. Throughout the entire world, the Roman government and the Roman army helped set the stage for the coming of Christ.

The intellectual contributions of the Greeks further set the stage for the revelation of Christ. The universal Gospel was in need of a universal language if it were to make a maximum impact on the world. Most Romans knew both Greek and Latin. Throughout the empire, everyone understood Greek as a common business language of the world.

Another picture to illustrate the importance of a common language can be seen in the developments following the destruction of the former Soviet Union. When the Russians occupied the huge territory of the Soviet Union, which encompassed over 390 million people, they spoke approximately 120 different languages. However, because of Russian occupation, all of the peoples that had been swallowed up in the Soviet Union were forced to speak and read Russian. This has been a great advantage to spreading of the Gospel throughout this region of the New World. Nearly 400 million people throughout this vast area read and speak Russian. Thus, Bible teachers and translators only need to translate materials into one language, rather than 120. Throughout the former Soviet Union, people desperately hungry to receive the Gospel and learn about the things of God can see and hear through one common language.

Greek philosophy further prepared the nation for the coming of Christianity by destroying the older religions. Both Socrates and Plato in the 5th century before Christ taught that this present temporal world and the senses are a mere shadow of the real world in which the highest ideals are intellectual abstractions. These abstractions included such things as: goodness, beauty, truth, etc. They taught that abstract virtues were more important than day-to-day existence.

The Greek philosophy systematically destroyed their beliefs in polytheistic worship. Their gods did not work. Therefore, they became more receptive to new information and revelation.

There were also many religious contributions made by the Hebrew people. Of foremost importance to Christianity is Hebrew monotheism — the belief in one and only one God. Further, in prophetic literature, one can find the Messianic hope...an incredible belief that the time of the Messiah was near. Many people, including the Pharisees of Jesus' day, held onto a strong hope in a coming Messiah. The Sadducees, the more political arm of Judaism, sought a political solution to the troubles of the Roman Empire. Thus, they viewed the time in which they lived as ripe for the Messiah to come. This Messiah, whether a religious or political leader, would be the One to deliver the people from their present circumstances.

The Hebrews also carried a very strong ethical system of law, which created true community. Along with the moral laws of the Torah (the Pentateuch), the Talmudic writings created specific rules governing all of life. Though these laws (especially the latter) were often trite and constricting, they created a community with similar cultural beliefs and moral values. The moral laws provided by God are still applicable to life today, though the Talmudic laws are far less applicable. It is true that Christians are not under the law, but under grace. The law that Jesus was referring to was the numerous ridiculous rules and regulations that kept people from worship, and from adequately following the Mosaic laws or the covenant of God. The moral law is still intact and must be understood to create a strong sense of community.

Further, Hebrews had the fullness of Old Testament scripture. These were read and meditated on, seen as light, important for the lives of their people. As individuals and as a community, they had a strong sense of destiny and history. They were/are God's chosen people. All of history hinged upon their activity in the world.

Conclusion

The unfolding of God's plan is seen in the history of the children of Israel. As the people of God, they had an awareness of their prophesied destiny, yet were captive to the Roman government and, in many ways, the Greek philosophy. In the midst of their despair, God in His infinite mercy and compassion sent Jesus to this world. Jesus was/is the plan, purpose and pattern ("*the Word became flesh,*" John 1:14) for all of life and ministry, the true Spiritual Architect of the Church.

End of Chapter Questions

Chapter Four

1. What three things did Ezra do to show us a pattern? (Ezra 7:10). Explain how this is done.
2. Explain the different mindsets of the Western and Eastern Christian.
3. How can the Church of today become community centers for the teaching of Christ and the pattern for church growth?
4. What occupations were the children of Israel involved in and who supervised them before the Exodus?

Chapter Five

The Jesus Pattern I

Teacher From God

The background described in Chapter 4 helped set the stage for the coming of Jesus. Jesus was born into a world filled with chaos, difficulty and distress. The Roman occupation, with its massive build-up of infrastructure, Greek philosophy and common language, established the foundation for change. For our purposes, the stage was set for the One to come Who would have the power to bring a message to the community of faith so desperately needed, a message of hope that would release them from their bondage of sin (Luke 4:1).

Throughout Palestine, as depicted in many of the Talmudic writings of the day, there was a tremendous anticipation that the disbursed children of Israel, scattered due to their sin and wickedness, would be gathered again, and that Israel would regain the prominence enjoyed under the reigns of King David and his son, Solomon. Much of this is discussed in the apocalyptic class of literature, the *Pseude Pigrapha*, including such books as *Enoch* and *Sibylline Oracles*. This anticipation of One Who would bring deliverance to the children of Israel and reestablish the throne of David was imminent.

Jesus was brought onto the scene for such a time as this.[5]

Jesus came to this earth at a very specific time, for a strategic purpose. His identity and purpose is revealed throughout scriptures. His interaction with Nicodemus provides a beginning of His purposeful pattern.

---
[5] "The Life and Times of Jesus, The Messiah," Alfred Edersheim, Ph.D., McDonald Publishing, McLean, VA, pgs. 78, 80.

In John 3:1-2 it says,

> "Now there was a man of the Pharisees named Nicodemus, a ruler of the Jews. This man came to him by night and said to him, Rabbi, we know that you have come from God for a teacher for no one can do these signs that you do unless God is with him."

Jesus came to teach and then to do.

The pattern demonstrated in Jesus' ministry was the pattern He learned from the prophets and was somewhat akin to the rabbinical tradition of the day. In Acts 1:1, the Apostle Luke presents this truth in opposite order (do and teach). Jesus frequently healed and then taught, but more often he taught and then healed. Signs following the teaching of the Word was most common, but we must remain as flexible as Jesus. Teaching was first on a rabbi's agenda, followed by action (at least it was supposed to), to demonstrate the truth of the teaching.

The Bible says Jesus taught with an authority different from the standard rabbi.

"Rabbinism started with demand of outward obedience and righteousness and pointed to sonship as its goal; the Gospel started with the free gift of forgiveness through faith and of sonship and pointed to obedience and righteousness as its goal."[6]

Jesus seemed to teach from a place of inside knowledge. He knew the essence of the heart and mind of the Father and presented His truths which did not contradict the law, but fulfilled it or explained it from the Father's perspective.

Nicodemus states what everyone in the time of Christ knew of Him: Jesus was an anointed, powerful teacher of God's Word. Nicodemus discerned that He must have come from God because of the demonstration of the power of God through signs, wonders and miracles, and the authority under which Jesus taught.

---

[6] "The Life and Times of Jesus, The Messiah," Ibid. pg. 106.

Jesus neither argued nor evaded the title He received. It was quite accurate. He was a teacher sent from God. Yet, more than a simple rabbi. He was one who could explain the law and the prophets from an insider's point of view.

Jesus came to proclaim and demonstrate a plan.

God is a God of plan. Before anything was, all things were contained in God, and God needed nothing. God does not need us, we need Him.

God creates from a place of order. The Trinity is a picture of the unity, the order of all life. All life follows a plan or purpose, and God's hand of design can be seen in every part of His creation. God is not the God of chaos but of order.

God is a God of purpose. His purpose was to create the world and place man in it, free to worship Him. God has been accused of being self-centered, demanding everyone to worship Him. That would only be true if God was anything less than God. God is not a man; God is God. He is absolutely perfect in love and purpose. He understands that the highest form of our good is to be a worshipper of Him.

God is a God of design. His design is for the communication of the Good News of Jesus Christ through the Church.

Jesus must have been highly skilled in His craft. He had experienced years of His own preparation, not just in terms of religious instruction, primarily at home and secondarily from His local synagogue in Nazareth, and through apprenticeship as a carpenter, living life amongst the covenant people of God.

When Jesus emerged into personal ministry there was something uniquely different about Him. The people of Galilee had already received the prophetic word from John; "One is coming." John came preaching repentance and baptism, an abhorrent thing to the Jews. Baptism was only for Gentiles, for the apostate, not for the covenant people of God.

So when John urged, "Repent and be baptized," he was saying that all were outside of the covenant of God. This was hard to hear for the prideful Jews. Yet, according to the Word of God, his message was well received, for *"all of the country of Judea...and Jerusalem were coming to Him"* (Matthew 1:5). John was anointed to preach this powerful message, and had a powerful and effective ministry. But, he was not specifically a teacher, and he did not come to build a movement. John primarily came, to fulfill his call and destiny — to be a forerunner of the One to come. In the life and ministry of John, he was willing to decrease so that Christ might increase. He understood his call and anointing, and he stayed within it, which is one of the keys to being effective in ministry.

Jesus began His ministry as a rabbi, coming from a place of obscurity, from a town of dubious reputation: Nazareth. He was not a mixer with the high and powerful, though He could hold His own in any social arena. Christ could have presented Himself in a number of ways, but He chose to be a humble servant. He did not come as a prophet, a political or religious leader, but as a teacher.

This was His first and primary identity: Jesus was a teacher sent from God to impart principles of the Kingdom into a rag-tag band of followers who eventually, under the anointing of the Holy Spirit, would turn the world upside-down for God! A careful study of scriptures reveals that Jesus spent the first half of His ministry primarily with His disciples, teaching and imparting to them the Kingdom of God.

He focused His attention on the preparation of men for ministry.

The ministry of Jesus followed portions of the rabbinical process, transmitted with the Word of God from generation to generation. God's plan for the building and the establishment of the Church is found in the Jesus Pattern.

The Authoritative Teacher

Luke 4 is a parallel passage to Isaiah 61, a very important and familiar passage of scripture. There are several key points to consider as we review this scripture. *"Jesus returned to Galilee,* (after his time in the wilderness) *in the power of the Spirit,"* (Luke 4:14). If one does not traverse the wilderness, there will not be ministry in the power of the Spirit. Dealing with temptations and overcoming them is the step to God's power.

As a model to others, Jesus traversed the wilderness as an overcomer. Though weakened, maybe smelling of smoke from the fiery trial he had gone through, He carried an authority different from other rabbis. He went through forty days of fasting and overcame every onslaught of the enemy.

When He left the wilderness, He was a victor, coming in the power of the Spirit!

Jesus did not need the wilderness experience to prove He was God. He was God prior to the wilderness experience. He suffered under the temptations of the enemy to prove that we could overcome the temptations of the enemy as men.

Every teacher worth his or her salt must go through times of trial and testing...with varied success (none perfectly). It is impossible to walk in the authority Jesus expressed unless we are full of the Spirit of God. Even then, we can only minister according to the measure of faith that God has given us, within the gifting and calling on our lives.

The model we see in the ministry of Jesus was that He was a teacher with great authority. That authority was hard fought and won in the battle of the wilderness, but also was part of the Spirit without measure that flowed through His life. Teachers today must teach under the authority given by the Word of God and the anointing of the Holy Spirit. If we don't go through a wilderness process ourselves, where we grapple with the old self, we will never teach with authority in the fullness of the Spirit according to the measure of faith that God has given us in our gifting and calling.

In Luke chapter 4:14-15 the Word of God says,

"And news about him spread through all the surrounding district. He began teaching in their synagogues and was praised by all."

The praise of man is not always a good thing, nor is it always a good sign. Jesus came to Nazareth, the city where He had been raised, and as was His custom, He entered the synagogue. From the time He was twelve years of age, He had spent countless hours training there. Most likely, He was part of a weekly, in some cases perhaps even a daily, gathering at the synagogue to hear the teaching of the elders in leadership of the synagogue.

During the time of Jesus, the city of Nazareth was a small city. This is well documented through archeological digs in the cemetery in Nazareth. The oldest cemetery there, dating back to the time of Christ, could only accommodate a city of about three hundred people. Thus, everybody knew Jesus. For at least eighteen plus years He attended the synagogue. To the leaders, He was "just" Jesus, except this time it was somehow different...this time Jesus spoke in the power of the Spirit.

Jesus had been well prepared through the standard teaching question and answer methodology of the synagogue. Rarely were straight lectures a part of the norm; typically, scrolls would be taken out and read in a systematic fashion. Someone would be chosen from the leadership within the synagogue and designated to read the passage of scripture scheduled for that day. Then, they were encouraged to provide exhortation on the passage read.

This is precisely what Jesus does in this passage! He was apparently already recognized as a rabbi, and thus, as was quite common and expected, a traveling teacher, one who had come from that synagogue and was now returning to receive the opportunity to read the scripture. This activity was probably done by Jesus hundreds of times as He was growing up within the city of Nazareth. Every elder in the city shared in that blessed responsibility. Jesus stood to read.

"He entered the synagogue and stood up to read (Out of respect for the Word of God). *The Book of the prophet Isaiah was handed to him."*

Someone once asked me, "Why was the book handed to him?" My guess would be that it was the reading for the day. Of course, it was all orchestrated by God, a part of His plan to validate the teaching ministry of His Son.

Jesus stood, they handed the scrolls to Him, and He opened the book, finding the place where it was written:

"The Spirit of the Lord is upon me because He anointed me to preach the Gospel to the poor; he hath sent me to heal the brokenhearted, to preach deliverance to the captives, and recovering of sight to the blind, to set at liberty them that are bruised, To preach the acceptable year of the Lord. He closed the book, gave it back to the attendant and sat down and the eyes of all the synagogue were fixed upon him."

They were fixed upon Him, not because of His preaching. He had yet to preach. He simply stood and read the Word...but there was something different...He read with authority.

Jesus said, *"Today this scripture has been fulfilled in your hearing."* That statement was probably something that just bubbled out of him. He proclaimed, "I'm it. I am the long awaited Messiah, the Anointed One."

His statement was not very well received.

Nevertheless, Jesus taught and spoke with an authority and an anointing often missing in the Body of Christ. There are ministers who constantly teach without the revelation of God's Word and little anointing on their lives. It was His authority and anointing that convicted, and His boldness in proclaiming His identity that pushed the elders to action.

Authority and anointing are absolutely required if one is to participate in building the Kingdom of God. One must flow in the measure of the authority that the Spirit of God has given. Only authoritative teaching that flows from an intimate knowledge of God's Word will accomplish God's purpose.

The elders, incensed with Christ's proclamation, intended to throw Jesus over a cliff, then cover Him with rocks. The Bible says He walked through the midst of them and escaped. He squared His shoulders, as He had the authority to do, and walked through them unharmed.

It was not His time.

A People To Receive

Jesus came into a cultural situation of great desperation which left the people's hearts open to receive a radical new message. Many, including most of the disciples, had preconceived notions about what a Messiah would be like, most believing Him to be a conqueror of the oppressor. Thus, He would be a transformer of society, returning Israel to the glory days of King David and King Solomon.

Eventually, Jesus will fully and completely establish His Kingdom here on Earth through the victorious Church. Along with the establishment of His Kingdom, He has called all of His people to be well prepared to rule and reign with Him. Jesus focused a major portion of His teaching and preaching ministry on how to prepare to rule and reign.

However, His first coming was not for the full establishment of His earthly Kingdom. Unfortunately for many in the time of Christ, they did not understand the Messianic promises that had been given, primarily through the prophets Isaiah and Ezekiel.

Jesus came as a teacher who demonstrated the power of God. He was shown and known to be a man of God, one with special gifting because of the signs, wonders and miracles He produced. Many have emphasized the miracle ministry of Christ as His primary ministry. However, from my understanding of the scriptures, that was not His primary focus. His concentration was on ministering to His disciples, which included the twelve, and eventually was extended to the 70, and ultimately to the 500, with the purpose of preparing them to be powerful ministers of the Gospel of Jesus Christ for the next and subsequent generations.

Through His ministry, He imparted Himself into His disciples. Thus, when His time was finished, His apostles would be able to carry on the message He imparted to them to the next generation as empowered by the Holy Spirit. Much of Jesus' teaching was prophetic in nature. He was continuously preparing His disciples for the day He would no longer be with them, teaching for a future day and time. He did not teach just for the sake of teaching, or to hear the sound of His voice. His teaching was with a plan...to fulfill the purposes of the heart of the Father.

In John 5:19, Jesus makes a statement about Himself and His ministry. He says, *"I don't do anything except what I hear or see my Father do."* Jesus came to express the fullness of the plan and purpose of God, to prepare a people, even as Moses, to possess the inheritance provided through the cross.

Jesus' teaching ministry established the plan and purpose of God in His disciples. Once established and empowered by the Holy Spirit, they were able to carry that message to the ends of the Earth. There are many other scriptures which present this truth (Matthew 26:39; John 5:30; John 6:36, 8:28, 12:49, 14:10). All have the same basic message: Jesus gave to His disciples what His Father gave to Him, an impartation of truth, and a pattern for the fulfillment of God's plan. Everything Christ received from the Father, discussed in the counsel of their own will, from the very beginning of time, was given to the apostles. Jesus was not presenting anything new — He was teaching the fullness of the divine plan from the very beginning to His chosen followers.

His focus was teaching the revelation of Who He was and what were the plan and purpose of God. Many local churches have excellent teaching programs, but they lack the ability to fulfill a biblical mandate: to teach God's people the patterns of life.

To teach the mind, not the spirit, is the focus of much of the modern Church. Church leaders teach the soul, or in some cases the flesh, but rarely the spirit. Jesus wanted to impart into the depth of the spirit of men and women that followed Him the truth of Who He was and what He came to do. He wanted that truth, as seed being sown into their lives to grow, germinate, and ultimately transform every aspect of their being. Their mind, their will, their emotions, their body, their activities, their purpose in life would be completely changed into the will of God. A whole different race of mankind, called "the second Adam", would emerge, bringing back to man what God intended for them from the beginning of creation.

HIS METHOD

Jesus taught individuals; He taught large crowds (See Matthew 5:2). When He taught the crowds, He rarely taught easily understood doctrine. Rather, He taught broad concepts. He mesmerized the crowds through His authority and story telling.

When He taught specifically to His disciples, He made His teaching plain and clear. When conducting a mass meeting, He laid out large principles such as the Beatitudes (Matthew, chapter 5). He presented moral principles for living in the Kingdom of God. Though He taught the crowds, His primary focus was the teaching of His disciples. Matthew 4:18-20 says,

"And walking by the sea of Galilee, he saw two brothers. Simon who was called Peter and Andrew

his brother, casting a net into the sea for they were fishermen. And he said to them, 'follow me and I will make you fishers of men.' They immediately left the nets and followed him."

What a strange thing!

Why would professional fishermen just drop their nets and follow Jesus?

Some speculate that Jesus must have had such a powerful anointing that He mesmerized them to follow Him. I'm sure that was part of it. Or, could it be that they were primed for this moment, hoping for someone to follow? Perhaps the invitation of the Master to "be with Him" was sufficient to incite action (Mark 3:13-14).

Some theologians believe that Peter and Andrew were formally followers of John the Baptist, and had left John to return to fishing. Others speculate that they were already periodic followers of Jesus. Thus, they knew His ministry and were ready to follow this rabbi if called to do so.

Continuing in Matthew 4, verse 21:

"He saw two other brothers, James the son of Zebedee and John his brother, In the boat was Zebedee their father, mending their nets; and he called them. And they immediately left the boat and their father, and followed him."

They said good-bye to their family of origin; their priority of life was now a commitment to follow Christ.

"Jesus was going about in all Galilee, teaching in their Synagogues and proclaiming the Gospel of the kingdom and healing every kind of disease and every kind of sickness among the people" (Verse 23).

Notice the order.

Jesus went to the teaching centers where people gathered to learn the scriptures. He did not principally conduct mass evangelistic crusades; He primarily visited teaching centers where people were gathering for the purpose of learning. They were seekers of truth.

There is a key here in terms of ministry.

A leader's time is best spent ministering to those whose hearts are open to receive. Ministry to the hardhearted leads to burnout. If one is going to spend time seeking those who don't want to be taught, or don't want to be found, burn-out is certain. If one teaches those that want to receive, great success is inevitable. Jesus did minister to the "whosoever will." In other words, if someone happened to be in His path, whoever it was, while He was moving from one synagogue to the next, He would minister as led by His Father. There were times when Jesus stopped to illustrate a principle for His disciples, but primarily He traveled from teaching place to teaching place, proclaiming the Gospel of the Kingdom.

The Good News that the Kingdom of God was in their midst was a bold statement to make. Jesus understood what He was declaring. "I am that I am. I am the Messiah."

That shocked many.

It confused some.

But His disciples were excited, thrilled that the Messiah was here. "Could this really be the One that we have been waiting for?," they would ask each other. Jesus proclaimed the Kingdom, and then demonstrated the Kingdom by healing and casting out demons. By destroying the works of darkness, He established the Father's reign on Earth.

THE TRANSFERENCE

This was the pattern He demonstrated to His disciples. Notice again that His priority was teaching. The teachings were to those that were seekers of truth. Jesus ministered to skeptics, to those who had studied Greek philosophy, leaders of the Roman government, and scholars of the law. There were Pharisees, Sadducees and the Hasidic. However, it was to the hungry and thirsty seekers of truth that Jesus stood to teach with a proclamation of power. He taught with an authority that was different from the other rabbis of the day, an authority validated by signs and wonders following.

Jesus taught for the purpose of establishing Kingdom service (see Matthew 10:1-5). He provided room for His disciples to grow in ministry. He instructed them before He sent them out. Matthew 10:1 says:

> *"And having summoned his twelve disciples, he gave them authority over unclean spirits. To cast them out and to heal every kind of disease and every kind of sickness."*

In verse 5 it further adds: *"These twelve Jesus sent out after instructing them saying..."*

Jesus instructed His followers to do as they had observed Him do.

By this time, Jesus' disciples had been with Him for a season of time. They had heard much of the basic doctrine of the Kingdom. *"Love your neighbor as you love yourself"* and various other moral principles were presented. They had seen Jesus and His ministry "up close and personal." They observed Him heal the sick, cleanse the lepers and open blind eyes.

They witnessed how Jesus did it!

In the right time and season, Jesus transferred a portion of His authority to His disciples. When they followed the pattern given, the same results as Christ were manifested. You can transfer authority if you first possess it. That's why you must obtain it first through an impartation of one to another.

The disciples had followed Jesus sufficiently for them to begin to think like Him, react like Him, probably even look and smell a bit like Him. We tend to become like the ones with whom we affiliate. They were modeled into a community, with Jesus as their leader, who was continuously, daily imparting to them revelation truth as well as developing fellowship together as brothers in the Lord.

When Jesus sent His disciples out into ministry, He established clear instructions so there would be no confusion as to what He expected from them. It is an unfortunate truth that many leaders will teach workers, imparting knowledge which lacks the proper guidance needed to understand what is expected. Most people need significant guidance from the leader to ensure that they can minister with confidence and fulfill the vision and purpose God has intended for them.

Jesus understood that the disciples were unskilled in ministry, even though they had been with Him. One might imagine that the disciples were excited to be released to do something for God. Yet, at the same time, they were most likely filled with doubt and fear. They were common folks with limited theological training. But they knew what Jesus said to them: "You have the authority."

They went forth in that authority, and it worked.

One item missing in ministry development strategies is cogent instruction from someone who knows what they are doing. Tommy Barnett uses the phrase, "Find a need and fill it — that is ministry."

True. But if you were actually to sit in with Pastor Barnett's leaders and observe the planning process before launching a ministry, you would see that there is more to the story. They do find the need, then find someone who has a burden for it, and after a significant time of instruction and development, that person is released into an area of leadership. Most assuredly, they take all the necessary steps to insure that the person to be sent is qualified, trained and has the necessary resources for success.

Jesus used the same basic pattern.

If we follow the patterns of the Lord, we will be successful in what He calls us to do.

End of Chapter Questions

Chapter Five

1. By what title was Jesus primarily known? Why is this significant?
2. What four characteristics of God are presented in this chapter? Describe each.
3. What did the wilderness experience produce in Christ? What lesson can we learn from this?
4. What did Jesus mean by His statement, *"Today this scripture has been fulfilled in your hearing"*?
5. Describe the primary method of Jesus' ministry.
6. What did Jesus transfer to His disciples?

Chapter Six

The Jesus Pattern II

Type Of Instruction

Matthew 13:3 provides a pictures of Christ's parabolic method of teaching. Jesus told many stories. He used parables to illustrate His principles. Frequently, the common person listening to Jesus did not understand His meaning. In teaching, a picture is really worth a thousand words. Jesus created pictures for people that would illustrate principles of the Kingdom.

One such picture is seen in the story of the mustard seed. Everyone in those days knew what a mustard seed was, and what a mustard seed became. Leaven in a lump of bread was understood by all (It causes the dough to expand). The Kingdom of God is always expanding. It starts from a small seed, but expands, grows and becomes huge, thousands of times greater than when it began.

Many of those listening felt, "Wow, what a fascinating story," but did not comprehended the full meaning. Neither did His intimate friends. Therefore, Jesus took His disciples off to the side, speaking to them plainly concerning the Kingdom of God and the meaning of His instruction. After all, those chosen by the Lord to be part of a leadership team deserve to receive clear and cogent instructions.

Conversely, clear instructions are not for those who are merely observers of the happenings of the Kingdom of God. They are reserved for those who have made a strong commitment to be followers of Christ and leaders of His Church. Jesus often used stories for the common person and for the general public, but then taught plainly to those who had been called to be with Him. Jesus was committed to their understanding of the fullness of His meaning.

Ultimately, they would be responsible for carrying the message that Jesus gave them to the next generation.

In Matthew 16:21, the Bible indicates that the great purpose of Jesus became revealed. Up until this point in the book of Matthew, Jesus primarily taught and demonstrated the Kingdom of God. Just prior to this Word in the 21st verse, and Jesus' new emphasis on His need to go to the cross and the resurrection, He had fed 4,000 people! Further, Peter had made the incredible proclamation that Jesus was the Christ, the Son of the Living God. Jesus spoke to Him, in the 18th verse, that upon this rock, upon the rock of the revelation that Jesus is the Christ, the Son of the Living God, that Jesus would build His Church and the gates of Hades would never overpower it.

Then He transferred to them the keys to the Kingdom to permit that which is in heaven to be done on Earth...another part of the pattern.

There comes a time in ministry when a leader is teaching, praying and working with God's people, ministering to those needy and hurting, when suddenly they seem to grasp the fullness of Who Jesus really is, what He came to do, and what their relationship is to Him. It is as though the Spirit of Revelation comes to them and they begin to fully understand what the Christian life involves:

- An understanding of salvation,
- A revelation on what Kingdom living is all about,
- An awareness that they are now an integral part of the Body of Christ with a position, a purpose and a destiny.

At this point real teaching begins...a teaching of depth designed to bring substance into the life of the believer. This is essentially what occurred in this juncture of Jesus' teaching ministry.

Up until this time, everything had been preliminary, setting the stage for them to understand the full revelation of His purpose and the Father's plan from the beginning of time. Now it was time to focus on an even greater preparation of discipleship where they would understand that they were to carry the message of this revelation to the next generation. In the 21st verse it says,

> *"From that time Jesus began to show to His disciples that He must go to Jerusalem, and suffer many things from the elders and chief priests and scribes, and be killed, and be raised the third day."*

In most church life, the focus is on recruiting as many people as possible to services. Leaders often seek numbers rather than quality followers. But it is faithfulness over time that equals success. Most of the great churches that exist today have become "overnight successes" after ten to fifteen years of faithful ministry. That may sound like a peculiar way to phrase, but it is true. Most churches start with little but are faithful to what God has said. Over time, God brings about the growth of His Kingdom.

Jesus remained faithful to His disciples. He imparted to them, over a period of only three-and-a-half years, preparing them for greater success than He experienced. Even though they didn't fully comprehend all Jesus meant until after the day of Pentecost, the full revelation came when the pattern and authority was mixed with the power and Spirit of God. In verse 21 it says,

> *"From that time, Jesus Christ began to show his disciples that he must go to Jerusalem and suffer many things from the elders and chief priests and scribes and be killed and be raised up on the third day."*

Peter became upset with God's plan, so He rebuked Jesus, misunderstanding the prime message. Ultimately what Jesus was saying was "What I must go through, you too must go through." Everything Jesus said or did was for their example. Peter did not look forward to the cross because He did not understand the plan. His natural view of success stood in the way of his ultimate purpose.

This is typical of the Church today.

We have listened to dynamic teaching, attempted to follow patterns that seem to work in terms of worldly success, yet we so often miss the very plan and purpose of God. The questions we must ask ourselves as leaders seem evident:

How do we build the Church?

How do we build the Kingdom of God?

My sense is, to do so, we must follow the methods found throughout all of biblical history, but especially those demonstrated through the life and ministry of the Lord Jesus Christ, then subsequently fine-tuned through the ministries of Peter and Paul.

Jesus said, "We must go to Jerusalem." Jesus was building for the next generation. Someone once said, "The Church is one generation away from extinction." This is always a possible truth. If we are not continuously raising up new disciples with a focus on winning the lost in the next generation, then the Church will most likely cease to exist.

This is true of any movement.

Over the past few years, the Church has missed much of their mandate because of the "escapist mentality" characterized by statements such as, "It's just Jesus and me," or "Lord, get me out of here. Let the rapture happen now."

Yes, the Lord is returning for His Church, but I am thoroughly convinced He is returning when this Gospel has been preached to every people group as a sign and testimony. It is then that the end will come. We all hope that the Lord will return in our lifetime (especially the older we get!), but God's intention for us is to build, establish and expand the Kingdom of God by following the patterns we find in the Word of God, thus fulfilling God's intention for our lives.

The Jesus Pattern II

The Practical

Jesus taught on very practical subjects (see Mark 10:1-12), including divorce and marriage, stewardship, the importance of basic relationships, and the need for forgiveness and restoration of those that have experienced broken relationships. Jesus taught both the theological and the practical, always with a specific purpose in mind (See Matthew 18).

To summarize: Jesus' teaching was both to the masses, which was often mystical, parabolic and difficult to understand. Further, He taught formally in the synagogue, and taught His disciples specifically and plainly. Jesus seemed to take His disciples from one level of revelation to another as they were able to understand. He always stretched them a little beyond their level of comprehension. With a new convert, we must start by teaching the simple and then bring them into the deeper principles of the Word of God.

Finally, He taught them in the very practical areas of life. His teaching methodology was more than just a method. Jesus was a master teacher sent from the Father Who taught with authority and with the purpose of impartation of a revelation that would carry His disciples to the next generation.

End of Chapter Questions

Chapter Six

1. By what means did Jesus teach? What was His purpose for doing so?
2. What was different about Jesus teaching the disciples versus the teaching to the crowds?
3. What was the "full revelation" of the Jesus Plan?
4. In what ways was Jesus' teaching practical and applicable?

Chapter Seven

The Jesus Pattern III

The Good Shepherd

"The LORD is my shepherd; I shall not want.

He makes me to lie down in green pastures; He leads me beside the still waters.

He restores my soul; He leads me in the paths of righteousness For His name's sake.

Yea, though I walk through the valley of the shadow of death, I will fear no evil; For You are with me; Your rod and Your staff, they comfort me.

You prepare a table before me in the presence of my enemies; You anoint my head with oil; My cup runs over.

Surely goodness and mercy shall follow me All the days of my life; And I will dwell in the house of the LORD Forever" (Psalm 23).

This particular Psalm is perhaps the most familiar passage of scripture known to man. Most of us know, either from previous instruction or by intuition, that each and every detail of this Davidic Psalm refers to Jesus Christ.

What may not be as apparent is that the model of shepherding relayed in the Old Covenant is the pattern for us in the Church age as well!

From this Psalm we can gather specific knowledge about what a true shepherd looks like! Of course, He looks a lot like Jesus! Jesus modeled true servant-leadership, as seen in the life of a true shepherd.

A true shepherd causes His sheep to be at rest, brings calmness and stillness to their lives.

He restores the sheep's thinking processes on an individual basis. Notice the singular and possessive pronouns used in the Psalm: my, I, He, me and so on. The word "shepherd" is singular, not plural. A true shepherd will always make some degree of personal and individual shepherding his or her top priority.

Notice the true shepherd "leads" in paths of righteousness; leading, not driving, is necessary.

A real shepherd does not desert the sheep when they are in sin or failure. In fact, a shepherd will stick with the sheep as they pass through the valley of the shadow of death. Even though sin brings the shadow of death to the sheep, a true shepherd refuses to desert the sheep. It is false to say that, "A true shepherd would never fellowship with people who are living in sin."

The rod in the hands of a true shepherd represents His guidance and provision, both necessary components. A true shepherd will be concerned with feeding the sheep, even when they are facing difficult and negative issues in their own day-to-day lives. "In the presence of my enemies" means just that — sin, weakness, corruption and failure are enemies, as are the demonic and worldly pressures to sin. True shepherds do not desert the sheep when the enemy is found within the sheep's lives. Always remember, Jesus ate and drank with the publicans and sinners; He did not even reject prostitutes.

Leaders are no better than the Son of God.

A shepherd too good for sinners is no shepherd at all.

There is an anointing that flows from the shepherd to the sheep that causes overflowing abundance. Goodness, mercy and the Presence of God flow from the life of a true shepherd, eternally abounding in the lives of His sheep on an individual and corporate basis. These characteristics can be a significant challenge for a pastor or leader in the Body of Christ, but Ephesians 5:1-2 tells us:

"Therefore be imitators of God as dear children. And walk in love, as Christ also has loved us and given Himself for us, an offering and a sacrifice to God for a sweet-smelling aroma."

We are to imitate the example Christ set for us. It is all too easy to forget our roles as leaders within the Church. Jesus said of His exemplary life and ministry:

"I am the good shepherd. The good shepherd gives His life for the sheep. But a hireling, he who is not the shepherd, one who does not own the sheep, sees the wolf coming and leaves the sheep and flees; and the wolf catches the sheep and scatters them. The hireling flees because he is a hireling and does not care about the sheep. I am the good shepherd; and I know My sheep, and am known by My own. As the Father knows Me, even so I know the Father; and I lay down My life for the sheep. And other sheep I have which are not of this fold; them also I must bring, and they will hear My voice; and there will be one flock and one shepherd" (John 10:11-16).

The word "pastor" itself means shepherd.

From that nurturing, pastoral example, set down by our Lord Jesus, we can ascertain and perceive His standards for those in leadership today! All shepherds are to be "good" in all that the term implies. Good shepherds, according to Jesus, will both live and die for the sheep.

Prior to the time Jesus ascended to the right hand of God, He gave some very pastoral commands to the men that would be leading His flock. We see His poignant interaction, with one in particular in John 21:15-17:

"So when they had eaten breakfast, Jesus said to Simon Peter, 'Simon, son of Jonah, do you love Me more than these?' He said to Him, 'Yes, Lord; You

know that I love You.' He said to him, 'Feed My lambs.' He said to him again a second time, 'Simon, son of Jonah, do you love Me?' He said to Him, 'Yes, Lord; You know that I love You.' He said to him, 'Tend My sheep.' He said to him the third time, 'Simon, son of Jonah, do you love Me?' Peter was grieved because He said to him the third time, 'Do you love Me?' And he said to Him, 'Lord, You know all things; You know that I love You.' Jesus said to him, 'Feed My sheep.'"

Much has been taught about the different words for "love" used by Jesus in this intimate exchange, as well as the differences between tending and feeding sheep. What can be lost in such teachings is the overall emphasis Jesus placed on the necessity to <u>imitate Him</u> in being a real "shepherd" to the flock of God. The message was not lost on Peter; years later, when Peter was approaching his life's end, he reiterated to others the very same command Jesus had given him personally! He said:

"Shepherd the flock of God which is among you, serving as overseers, not by compulsion but willingly, not for dishonest gain but eagerly; nor as being lords over those entrusted to you, but being examples to the flock; and when the Chief Shepherd appears, you will receive the crown of glory that does not fade away," (I Peter 5:2-4).

It is apparent that the disciples of Jesus, especially those called to five-fold ministry offices, are to fulfill the shepherding role as a primary function. Regardless of the titles assigned, ministry leadership is to strive to fulfill the many roles of shepherding. These include:

- Nurture: This is the role of giving care, feeding, sustaining and the demonstration of God's grace by exhibiting His unconditional love.
- Teach: The Word of God is taught by word of mouth as well as demonstration through personal example! "Do what I say, not as I do" is not allowed here.

- Disciple: This involves mentoring others sacrificially. We are challenged to develop disciples for ministry and then send them out to do their part in the Body of Christ.
- Build Relationships: Horizontal relationships allow us to be built together, and to flow God's grace to one another. The methods and practices for building a vertical relationship with God and horizontal relationships with one another are to be developed and maintained vigorously.
- Set The Pace: More than being in front, leadership at its finest is leadership by example.
- Edify: Build up His Body by building up individuals, personally and actively.
- Exhort: Encouragement in lieu of commandments. Government by praise instead of edict. Enablement and empowerment to succeed will produce success. Jesus called His people His sheep for good reason.

Though sheep may be dirty and unkempt, the shepherd still loves and cares for them. Sheep are not always the most brilliant; they can easily be led astray. Still, the shepherd loves and cares for them. Sheep can wander away, encountering serious danger. Still, the shepherd loves and cares for them. Sometimes sheep become injured through their disobedience. Still, the shepherd loves them, cares for them, binds their wounds and carries the most severely injured of them on his/her capable shoulders.

It bears repeating: Only those who truly love the sheep and the great Shepherd will find pleasure in doing the sometimes dirty and often thankless job of shepherding God's Flock.

A Hireling? A False Shepherd?

Scripture speaks about another kind of shepherd, one who does not care for the sheep. Again:

> *"I am the good shepherd. The good shepherd gives His life for the sheep. But a hireling, he who is*

not the shepherd, one who does not own the sheep, sees the wolf coming and leaves the sheep and flees; and the wolf catches the sheep and scatters them. The hireling flees because he is a hireling and does not care about the sheep,'"* (John 10:11-13).

A hireling shepherd tends the sheep for personal profit, acclaim, monetary gain or other inappropriate motivations. He will not make true sacrifice for the sheep. He will not lay down his own life, his own desires and ambitions for the good of God's flock. When a member of the shepherd's family tends the flock, the entire family relationship becomes involved in the sheep-tending and raising endeavor.

There is a living and vital difference between a hireling shepherd and a good shepherd. Scripture goes well beyond the hireling category in its characterization of shepherds. There are also "wolves" in sheep's clothing, evil shepherds as well as false shepherds. None are worthy of following; they cannot be trusted. God is committed to protecting His sheep from them. He will take great measures to deliver His sheep from the destruction that these evil shepherds wreak upon the lives of His flock!

The prophets Jeremiah, Isaiah and Ezekiel had much to say about these evil characters, and their words came straight from God's heart, the Great Shepherd Himself! From their unique prophecies we can learn even more about shepherds and sheep.

"'But I will gather the remnant of My flock out of all countries where I have driven them, and bring them back to their folds; and they shall be fruitful and increase. I will set up shepherds over them who will feed them; and they shall fear no more, nor be dismayed, nor shall they be lacking,' says the LORD," (Jeremiah 23:3-4).

Here we see that God desires His sheep to stay in the fold so that they can be fruitful and increase. Any "fold" where sheep are not being fruitful and experiencing increase is suspect for not being a real "fold" at all! We also can gather that proper shepherding removes fear, dismay and lack form the lives of the sheep. An abundance of any of these negative forces is a further indication that true shepherding is not taking place.

> *"'Wail, shepherds, and cry! Roll about in the ashes, You leaders of the flock! For the days of your slaughter and your dispersions are fulfilled; You shall fall like a precious vessel. And the shepherds will have no way to flee, Nor the leaders of the flock to escape. A voice of the cry of the shepherds, And a wailing of the leaders to the flock will be heard. For the LORD has plundered their pasture, And the peaceful dwellings are cut down because of the fierce anger of the LORD,'"* (Jeremiah 25:34-37).

Here we see God's commitment to expose evil shepherds who are exploiting His sheep. Many leaders, some with ulterior motivations in their ministries, have been weeded out in recent years. This will be a continuing trend if change and righteous motivation is not sought by the next generation of leaders. The Great Shepherd's first concern is the condition of His sheep. And, He connects their condition directly to the responsibilities and job performance of the shepherds who are tending them!

Despite all the negatives we have seen and experienced, we as His sheep can look forward to a soon-coming brighter day. For God said:

> *"Thus says the LORD of hosts: 'In this place which is desolate, without man and without beast, and in all its cities, there shall again be a dwelling place of shepherds causing their flocks to lie down. In the cities of the mountains, in the cities of the lowland, in the cities of the South, in the land of Benjamin, in the places around Jerusalem, and in the cities of Judah, the flocks shall again pass under the hands of him who counts them,' says the LORD,"* (Jeremiah 33:12-13).

God is truly committed to restoring the shepherd/sheep relationship where it has gone awry. And, He will hold individual shepherds accountable for the devastation in the sheep's lives:

> *"My people have been lost sheep. Their shepherds have led them astray; They have turned them away on the mountains. They have gone from mountain to hill; They have forgotten their resting place. All who found them have devoured them; And their adversaries said, 'We have not offended, Because they have sinned against the LORD, the habitation of justice, The LORD, the hope of their fathers,'"* (Jeremiah 50:6-7).

Perhaps the most complete instance of God confronting the false shepherd is found in Ezekiel 34:5-12:

> *"So they were scattered because there was no shepherd; and they became food for all the beasts of the field when they were scattered. My sheep wandered through all the mountains, and on every high hill; yes, My flock was scattered over the whole face of the earth, and no one was seeking or searching for them. Therefore, you shepherds, hear the word of the LORD: 'as I live, says the Lord GOD, surely because My flock became a prey, and My flock became food for every beast of the field, because there was no shepherd, nor did My shepherds search for My flock, but the shepherds fed themselves and did not feed My flock. Therefore, O shepherds, hear the word of the LORD! Thus says the Lord GOD: 'Behold, I am against the shepherds, and I will require My flock at their hand; I will cause them to cease feeding the sheep, and the shepherds shall feed themselves no more; for I will deliver My flock from their mouths, that they may no longer be food for them.' For thus says the Lord GOD: 'Indeed I Myself will search for My sheep and seek them out. As a shepherd seeks out his flock on the day he is*

among his scattered sheep, so will I seek out My sheep and deliver them...'"

God's indictments against the shepherds include:
- They allowed His sheep to be scattered.
- They allowed the sheep to become easy prey to beasts that devour.
- The shepherds devoured the sheep instead of feeding and nurturing them for growth and fruitfulness so they could produce much-needed wool and offspring.
- They did not heal the sheep.
- They would not feed the sheep. The five-fold ministries would come under this category as well. The five ministries should be called in to help when the burden of feeding is too much to handle.

What is God's sentence against "greedy and disobedient" shepherds? He declares...

"You are fired!"

"You will no longer be provided for!"

"You will never again eat up MY sheep!"

GOD'S PLAN FOR RESTORATION

God sent Jesus as the Good Shepherd Who continues to do the following through each under-shepherd He appoints. You will find each of these areas in the very same passage of Ezekiel:

- I will personally search for and seek out the sheep that are Mine!

- I will deliver them, personally at My own effort and expense!
- I will bring them into their own land...their eternal, spiritual and material inheritance.
- I will feed them.
- I will provide them with rest in a good fold, with a rich pasture in the mountains. My Rest is not a heavy yoke of rules, regulations and obligations.

- I will make them lie down. Rest and recreation are the divine order of the day!
- I will heal their sick.
- I will bind up (or build up) the broken.
- I will destroy the rich and the fat — the false leaders who fed themselves gruesomely by killing and eating the flock.

God's Promise For Faithful Shepherds

God is committed to His sheep, as are good shepherds. Those called to leadership often have choices to make which are not always easy. They may lead to loss at times, and even death, but God's pattern is clear. He has not been vague about what He requires of His shepherds. He has not withheld from us His certified promise of immeasurable reward and provision, if we will but serve faithfully according to the pattern He has laid out for us.

"Shepherd the flock of God which is among you, serving as overseers, not by compulsion but willingly, not for dishonest gain but eagerly; nor as being lords over those entrusted to you, but being examples to the flock; and when the Chief Shepherd appears, you will receive the crown of glory that does not fade away" (I Peter 5:2-4).

It is the responsibility of an under-shepherd to faithfully minister to, guard and protect the sheep which have been placed in his/her care. It is only through faithfulness to the call of God within His Kingdom that the crown of life can be earned.

Teach For Fruit

John 15 talks about Jesus' focus on teaching to bring forth fruit. Jesus did not teach to impress, but to impart. He wanted His disciples to bear fruit. He taught to see change in His disciples that would carry on to the next generation.

Jesus taught that transformation comes when one dwells or lives in complete communion with the Word. The word for "Word" found in John 15 is not the "Rhema" of God, or "Graphe", it's the "Logos" of God or "the living Word." Thus, Jesus is stating that His Word, the plan, the purpose, the very thought, belief and identity of God is to abide in His disciples. He wanted the plan, the purpose, the vision, the prophetic to dwell in His apostles, which would allow them to experience a fruitful life of service.

This is what true prophetic ministry does.

Jesus was a prophetic teacher. He didn't teach just for today. He taught for today and forever. He provided, through His anointed teaching, a glimpse of tomorrow, a dream for the future. True prophetic ministry speaks a word that takes us from today into tomorrow, giving us a vision for the future.

Fortunately, God is gracious and rarely shows us what is between today and tomorrow. If He did, we probably would not want to take the journey. As is often the case, the valley of the shadow of death and many difficult experiences are in between the Word and its fulfillment.

Jesus stated, *"I want you to abide in My word and have My word abide in you so that you might bear much fruit."*

It has never been God's intention for His children to be barren. In context, Jesus is speaking about bearing many children...spirit children in the Kingdom. That's why every believer should be a soul winner, with a minimum goal of reaching and discipling at least one person a year.

Jesus taught the parable of the seeds and the sower. He explained that much of our seed will fall on barren ground. Some will get into rocky soil, some into shallow soil, but He promised us that what goes into good soil will bear much fruit.

THE ULTIMATE PURPOSE

In verse 18 it says, *"And Jesus came up and spoke to them saying, 'All authority has been given to me in heaven and in earth.'"* Reiterating what He stated back in Luke 4, He had the authority to do everything that He had done. *"Go therefore and make disciples of all the nations."* Notice again, it says go and make disciples, not converts. This is apostolic teaching, establishing a foundation of discipleship.

From converts come disciples. Salvation begins with a conversion experience. Jesus' focus of ministry was to make disciples, not just of individuals, but of whole nations or people groups. Further, those converted were to be baptized.

Baptism meant a full and complete identification with the Church, with the death, burial and resurrection of Jesus Christ. It was generally a public event, not in a private baptistery but in a public lake or stream. The public testimony declares, "I am choosing to follow the Master, to follow Christ."

Then Jesus continued, *"Teaching them to observe."* The word "observe" is not just "to view or to look at." It means "to both hear and to do." The commandment was to observe or do all that Jesus commanded, and in doing so, His presence was assured to be with them. True discipleship can only come through teaching all Jesus commanded, following the pattern He lived.

What did Jesus want His apostles to teach?

What they had learned, not just from study or reading, but also their learning from observation or experience. *"Teach everything that I have commanded you."* Who received this commission? The eleven. Now we also embrace this as our commission, at least in theory if not in action. But the commission was primarily given to His disciples.

The goal was to take the Gospel of the Kingdom to Jerusalem, Judaea, Samaria, to the uttermost parts of the earth, to make disciples, to develop others to be like them.

The apostles understood the commission, and followed it to their level of understanding.

END OF CHAPTER QUESTIONS

CHAPTER SEVEN

1. What particular qualities are prerequisite for taking a leadership position in the Church besides the obvious ones of faithfulness, prayer and obedience?
2. Should a pastor/shepherd be more concerned with attending to the flock he or she has in the local church or reaching beyond (perhaps overseas) to gather and cultivate new flocks?
3. Did Jesus teach the same way to the crowds as to His disciples? Explain.
4. Describe the characteristics of a good shepherd and how they relate to those in leadership today.
5. Discuss the seven differing roles of shepherding.
6. What is a "hireling shepherd"?
7. What are the signs of a hireling shepherd's ministry?
8. What does the concept "teach for fruit" mean?

CHAPTER EIGHT

THE MISSION MANDATE

THE TRANSFER

In Matthew 28, Christ gave His disciples the Great Commission. Jesus presented His commission at the end of His earthly ministry, following His death and resurrection, after He had finished spending forty to fifty days teaching His disciples on various occasions, reiterating to them everything that He had taught them previously.

The importance of this last will and testament cannot be minimized.

His teaching is illustrated through the story of two men found on the Emmaus road. Scripture says, *"And beginning from the law and the prophets expounded to them everything concerning the Kingdom of God,"* (Luke 24:27). Jesus spoke to these men, as well as to His disciples, after His death and resurrection and before His ascension, imparting to them His final instructions. This was His last will and testament to His disciples.

When a person is on their death bed, they will often ask a loved one to do something specific for them. Those final words are not just simple requests, they amount to highly impactful commands. Also, when one reads the contents of a will, the requests go beyond mere thoughts, becoming a mandate to fulfill.

When Jesus spoke to His disciples, He was revealing His final instructions as a mandate for them. They took His words most seriously. Starting with Matthew 28:16, it says,

> *"But the eleven disciples proceeded to Galilee to the mountain which Jesus had designated. When they saw him, they worshipped him, but some were doubtful."*

Perhaps the disciples were doubtful about the reality of Jesus' bodily resurrection. If His own disciples, who had been with Him for three-and-a-half years, saw Him arrested in the garden, knew that He died on the cross, that He was no longer in the grave, who saw the nail prints and the hole in His side, still doubted, it should not surprise us that there are people, even members of the household of faith, that still carry a certain amount of doubt for a season.

Jesus' command to His disciples was to do all of the things that Jesus did, teach the ways He taught, command the way He commanded, live the way He lived.

In summary, do just like Him!

In Acts 1:4, Luke continues with the instructions of Christ: *"And gathering them together, he commanded them not to leave Jerusalem, but to wait for what the Father had promised."* This occurred at the same gathering presented in Matthew 28. Continuing, it says: *"You heard from me, for John Baptized with water but you shall be baptized with the Holy Spirit not many days from now."*

This was not the first time the disciples heard Jesus speak on Baptism, since He started to teach this when He first met His disciples after His baptism, after coming out of the wilderness in power. He taught on the Kingdom, which was empowered by being baptized in the Holy Spirit. They had been prepared for, and were looking for, this time to come. Jesus had breathed on them the Holy Spirit. They had gone out and ministered, but they never had the Holy Spirit fully on the inside like we experience the Holy Spirit today.

"So when they had come together, they were asking him saying 'Lord is it at this time you are restoring the kingdom of Israel?'" (Acts 1:6). These men had been with Jesus for three-and-a-half years. They had heard all of His teaching, seen the demonstration of signs, wonders and miracles. They had heard, "I'm going to the cross, I'm dying, and will rise again the third day. It's my vicarious, atoning death on the cross for all of mankind that brings salvation. The Holy

Spirit is coming to actually live inside you. God is going to be living and dwelling in the tabernacle of man, in earthen vessels."

After all of that, they still asked, "Are you going to set up your Kingdom now on the Earth? We are ready now. Come on Jesus let's do it."

They still lacked understanding!

They were still thinking in terms of the natural, not the spiritual!

It shouldn't surprise us if, after spending some significant time with people and seeing them nod their heads and say "yes," that they do not get it. I do not think these questions surprised Jesus.

He replied,

"It is not for you to know times or epics which the Father has fixed by his own authority, but you shall receive power when the Holy Spirit is come upon you. You shall be my martyrs both in Jerusalem, in all Judaea, Samaria and even to the remotest part of the earth" (Acts 1:7-8).

In context, He is not saying, "First start in Jerusalem and after you build your 1000 seat sanctuary, then Judaea, then reach all the way out to Samaria. Then once you have established a network of churches, and you are pulling in a ten percent tithe, plus offerings, and when you are able to build a massive missions fund, then start planting churches in the remotest parts of the earth."

Jesus said to do it all now.

Take the Gospel everywhere.

He stated this especially and specifically to His disciples. In chapter 2, we see the promise received. Jesus knew what His disciples needed to fulfill their call...authority and power (Spirit)! They could not do it in their own authority. Even with all the great teaching they had received, all the experience of being loved by God, experiencing Jesus, it was not enough. They needed "Dunamis"...true "power" on the inside flowing out for others, giving power to be martyrs (witnesses) for Christ.

End of Chapter Questions

Chapter Eight

1. What is the "Great Commission" in Matthew 28? How do you think the apostles were to fulfill this?
2. What are we, as Jesus' disciples of today, to do? Does the "Great Commission" apply to us today?
3. What did Jesus discuss with the two men on the Emmaus road?
4. What is the "Mission Mandate?"
5. What is the "Last will and testament of Jesus?"
6. What were the disciples waiting for?
7. What does it say about our society when a person's last will and testament is so revered and taken seriously regarding material things, but the last will and testament of our Lord Jesus Christ has been disregarded by so many?

Chapter Nine

The Downpour

The Day of Pentecost

After Christ commissioned the apostles, they were obedient to the command of God. They had faithfully waited, praying in unity, until the promise of the Lord came. When the Holy Spirit descended in power, there was a great commotion. The power of God filled the believers, providing them the ability to speak in languages understood by the populace of the city. The newly transformed believers boldly poured out into the street, proclaiming the glory of God, exclaiming that the Messiah, the Lord's Christ had come.

Thank God they were willing to tarry in the Upper Room to receive the promise. Many need that today. But also thank God they did not stay there, rejoicing in the blessings, but were willing to "hit the streets" and proclaim the revelation of Christ. Many of us need an Upper Room experience today, and many need to go beyond that wonderful experience into the streets as Jesus commanded.

Acts 2:5 is a very revealing scripture. It says, *"There were Jews living in Jerusalem. Devout men from every nation under heaven."*

Who were these people?

Devout Jews were in Jerusalem from all over the region.

What were they doing there?

The occasion of Pentecost coincided with the Feast of Pentecost. The devout men (and women) were there for this grand and glorious celebration occurring in Jerusalem during this time of the year. For most, this was a pilgrimage of the faithful, coming from throughout the known world for this sacred occasion.

For many, it was their annual pilgrimage to the temple. For some, it was the only time they had the privilege of temple worship.

What were they seeking?

They came to Jerusalem to worship God. Thus, they were seekers, hungry for God, visiting in Jerusalem to proclaim their devotion to God through temple worship.

During this feast, the city would swell with thousands of seekers. In the midst of temple worship, the 120 came rolling out of the Upper Room, speaking in languages that the visitors to Jerusalem understood. The words spoken proclaimed the Good News of the Kingdom!

Jesus is Messiah! He is risen!

It was then that some asked the question, "Are they drunk? Or, is this true?" Peter stood, preaching a very simple sermon; the timing was perfect. He powerfully proclaimed the message of the Gospel of the Kingdom.

The result?

3,000 souls were saved from that one message!

What dynamic church growth! Supernatural! Incredible!

INTRODUCTION TO THE FULLNESS OF THE KINGDOM

Dr. Wagner states in his commentary, *Lighting the World* (C. Peter Wagner, Regal Books Publication, 1995, pg. 19) that the Gospels are foundational to the experience of Pentecost. Jesus laid a strong, solid foundation for His apostles, based upon His own life and ministry. And, as stated before, His focus was on developing the life of the Kingdom of God through His apostles. Jesus knew that without the supernatural power of the Holy Spirit flowing through the everyday believer, the purposes of God and His own life would not be fulfilled.

In the Gospel of Luke, Jesus' foundational ministry is explained. The Book of Acts delineates all that Jesus expected His apostles and other followers to do, both for that day and now. Further, the Kingdom of God is the major theological framework for understanding the Book of Acts. The Book of Acts begins with the Kingdom of God and ends there. All that the apostles did pertained to the development and expansion of the Kingdom of God.

What is the Kingdom of God?

> "The Kingdom is present first and foremost wherever Jesus Christ is acknowledged and served as King. It is not a geopolitical territory with recognized boundaries. It could not join the United Nations. It is a Kingdom not of this world, but nonetheless it is in this world. It is essentially a spiritual Kingdom, but it also has tangible, visible manifestations" (Wagner, 2).

Jesus proclaimed the Kingdom of God and the apostles continued to do the same. The purpose of the establishment of the Kingdom of God was to bring to pass the rule and reign of Christ, which is both now and future. When the Holy Spirit came in power on the day of Pentecost, it released the apostles to begin the process of establishing the Kingdom of God wherever they went. Wherever the Gospel of Jesus Christ is proclaimed, where signs and wonders follow the preaching of the Word, it proclaims that the Kingdom of God is taking a foothold within that community. When the Apostle Peter stood on the day of Pentecost and preached that powerful message, he was proclaiming to all who could hear that the Kingdom of God is beginning here in Jerusalem. The sign that the Kingdom had come was the salvation of the 3,000 souls in one day.

Shortly thereafter, miracles began.

At the gate beautiful a crippled man was brought to his feet, entering the temple rejoicing at the grace and mercy of God. All miracles come through the power of the Holy Spirit as a continual extension of the ministry of Christ. Jesus' ministry can be summarized in Luke chapter 4, which is a paraphrase of Isaiah 61. He came to...

"...preach the Gospel to the poor, to heal the broken hearted, to preach deliverance to the captives, the recovery of sight to the blind, to set at liberty those who are oppressed and to preach the favorable year of the Lord."

Jesus began this anointed ministry after His baptism, continuing it through His apostles from the day of Pentecost. His ministry is to be part of the continuing work of the grace of God in and through the Church today.

As can be seen in Acts 2, whenever the Gospel is preached, problems happen. They occurred during Jesus' ministry, and prior to Christ. Anytime a prophet preached righteousness, holiness and commitment to the covenant of God, problems occurred. It seems that any ministry truly supernatural in focus is going to attract the wild and the wonderful, and will create conflict within the spiritual and natural realms.

This was certainly true in the 1st Century Church.

Shortly after the preaching of this wonderful message by the Apostle Peter, all of heaven rejoiced, but all hell broke loose. Problems manifested immediately and had to be addressed by the apostles, just as they have had to be addressed by God's leaders throughout Church history.

The day of Pentecost set in motion certain crises, which led to God's purposes for church growth and development being fulfilled. The first crisis, to be expanded in detail in the next chapter, was the explosive growth and logistics of gathering people who had received a common grace. As difficult as this must have been, it was an exciting time for the apostles. Clearly they were in their element. They had been trained for this very purpose. It turned their attention to training, teaching, equipping and ministering to the needs of those God had supernaturally birthed into the Kingdom.

But God had so much more in mind than a mono-cultural, Jewish Church. He wanted the entire world to know that *"...God so loved the world that He gave His only begotten*

Son, and that whosoever believeth in Him should not perish, but have everlasting life" (John 3:16). Thus, in spite of the mono-cultural worldview of the followers of Christ after the day of Pentecost, God had another crisis coming that would force Hebrew believers into a larger worldview, a perspective which would include all races and creeds, from every imaginable cultural background.

End of Chapter Questions

Chapter Nine

1. Why were there only 120 gathered in the Upper Room?
2. What was "The Promise" they received? What happened?
3. Who were the visitors in Jerusalem? Why is this significant?
4. What were the seekers doing in Jerusalem?
5. Who preached? Why is preaching so important in God's economy?

CHAPTER TEN

WHEN HEAVEN CAME DOWN: CRISIS ONE

There is such a difference preaching overseas!

On foreign soil, people are unspoiled by television, and are not damaged by religious familiarity. Their hearts are open; they are people ready to receive the truth of Jesus. In America, there are seekers, honest, open, desirous to know the truth of Christ. However, (for the most part) they are not in the pews or our home fellowships, but in the streets, amongst the outcast, with the gangs and the burnt out. May God help us call out to the seekers so they might find the water and bread of healing and restoration.

What an outstanding start for the Church of Jesus Christ. In one magnificent swoop, the Church grew from 120 to 3,120 (or more)...without a church building, programs, chairs, children's church, offering baskets or 501(c) 3's.

My Lord, what a mess! Where were these souls from?

Everywhere.

Did they live in Jerusalem?

Perhaps some had family in Jerusalem. Most had jobs in other communities. Many came to Jerusalem with whatever they could carry on their backs or donkeys.

Thus, the apostles had a dilemma on their hands. They must have thought, "We have all of these people who have just confessed faith in Jesus Christ as the Messiah. Isn't this exciting! Now what do we do with them?" The mandate Jesus had given was to teach and baptize them, making disciples of all nations.

But where were they going to put all of these people?

They had no permanent place to live, no jobs, no major resources, no building to meet in, and no baptistery. The promise of God was realized; the miracle was in the hearing of the Gospel in their own language. They were honest seekers. The power of God was released. The Church was born, and so was a tremendous problem. The apostles made a quality decision, instructing their new converts to stay in Jerusalem; the new believers obeyed.

Church history indicates that, from that day, the believers met on a daily basis on Solomon's porch, a large, open area behind the temple. There was no room for them in the temple itself what with all the other activities happening there. So they would meet in the back of the temple where the apostles would teach them "daily."

As we continue in chapter 2, it is apparent that the grace of God was especially on the people.

"And they were continually devoting themselves to the apostles teaching and to fellowship and the breaking of bread and to prayer" (verse 42).

These four common elements — teaching, fellowship, the breaking of bread, and prayer — should be a part of every fellowship gathering. As they gathered, the apostles taught the believers everything Jesus taught them. Of course, that is all they knew. They taught them on Solomon's porch and in private homes, the only places available to them at the time.

The logistics must have been unbelievable!

Imagine...they had 3,000 new Jewish converts! They had 120 leaders. These 120 would certainly show normal hospitality, attempting to house the 3,000. What an exciting thought! They must have asked, "Where are we going to stay?" They all decided to stay in Jerusalem rather than return home. They probably sent word to their families to join them, proclaiming the Good News that they had found the Messiah and eternal life. So, one of the ways the Church grew was by bringing Jewish believers out of the nations into Jerusalem.

The initial days, weeks and months must have been most exciting - a flurry of activity as they searched for housing, worked through conflicts caused by the housing problems, teaching at Solomon's Porch, temple worship, house meetings and work (to pay the bills.) The apostles were clearly in charge. After all, they had been trained by the Jewish Messiah, a Rabbi of rabbis, and now, by the power of the Holy Spirit, who brought back remembrance of all Jesus said and did, they were discipling their Jewish brothers and sisters in the truth of Jesus Christ.

One result of this tremendous outpouring was a change in heart and priority. Everyone was giving all they had, as the apostles did previously, to supply for the needs of the saints (except Ananias and Saphira, who disobeyed and experienced the powerful new authority of the Church), and favor was theirs within the Jewish community.

Who could ask for more?

God!

There are several observations one can make from reading the accounts of the early Church. The observations are open to interpretation: here are mine.

Notice there were no pastors, evangelists, prophets or teachers. There were simply apostles. Church life at its best should be founded upon apostolic and prophetic ministry. To have a solid foundation, an apostolic/prophetic ministry is essential. Pastors shepherd the sheep, but they rarely have the anointing or calling to establish foundationally a church. Ultimately, there should be five-fold ministry operating together. More on this later.

The Word of God was preached and souls were won. God's power was released. Miracles began to happen through the ministry of Peter and John.

The apostles' primary focus was on building a community of faith in Jerusalem. They apparently forgot their primary mandate. We understand why. They were busy. 3,000 came at one time, 5,000 a few days later. New converts, all Jews, were coming to the Messiah in droves! Families were moving in, finding jobs; the apostles were trying to make sure that all were cared for and fed. All of those tasks were handled by the eleven apostles and their assistants.

Then, the power of God was released and the promise of God led to prosperity. Acts 4:32-35 says:

> *"The congregation of those who believed were of one heart and soul and not one of them claimed that anything belonging to him was his own. But all things were common property to them. With great power, the apostles were giving witness to the resurrection of the Lord Jesus and abundant grace was upon them all. For there was not a needy person among them for all who were owners of land or houses would sell them and bring the proceeds of the sales and lay them at the apostles' feet. They would be distributed to each as they had need."*

Incredibly wonderful things were happening! A great Jewish sect was being developed where everyone was so devoted to the teachings of the apostles and to the life of Christ that they were willing to give up everything for them. This is the New Testament model of giving.

One can only imagine the excitement of the times. When the apostles taught about Jesus, they might have been asked, "Well, tell us Peter, what was it like in the beginning? What was it like when you first met Jesus? Give us your testimony." That was a most common activity in those days, and still quite common today. "Tell me your testimony. How did you come to know Christ?" Peter would have answered, "Well, I was out fishing with my brother and Jesus said, 'Come and I will make you a fisher of men.' And there was something about what He said. He captivated us so much that we left everything and followed Him." Andrew, Bartholomew, Matthew and the rest most likely answered in similar manner.

So what was the norm for a disciple of Jesus? To leave everything and follow Him. How far away we have wandered from that early Church expectation (not demand).

The apostles preached the truth of the Gospel and their experience within a comfortable Hebrew cultural context. Jesus had given everything, coming from His throne in glory to the earth. Therefore, that was the expectation of all. It made perfect sense for believers excited about life in Christ to put everything at the apostles' feet. They had no worries about trusting these men. Unfortunately, it becomes painfully clear that the apostles' understanding of the mandate of Christ was limited by their cultural worldview. Though numerous Old Testament scriptures familiar to the apostles speak of the nations being blessed, they were unable or unwilling (except for Cornelius) to cross-culturally minister the Gospel of Christ. As with many churches today, they only made contact with their own kind, not risking the social awkwardness of including groups of divergent ethnic roots.

How this must have grieved the heart of God.

He allowed it for a season, though not without purpose. Soon He would move them to a greater understanding of His plan from the ages.

The new converts were taught, trained and developed. God was blessing tremendously, and the momentum of the Church was growing and growing. Perhaps the apostles assumed that God's favor would last forever.

Though persecution was promised by the Lord (John 16:33), the success of their work and the load of their ministry must have been overwhelming. How easy it would be for any of us to forget or delay the vision of Christ for the glory of growth in our ministry. God's grace and mercy allowed their myopic focus of ministry. Of course, we cannot be critical of the apostles in Jerusalem. How many of us are guilty of the "My Jerusalem first" mentality? Soon, the stage would be fully set for the dissemination of the Gospel to the nations.

But first, another necessary crisis.

END OF CHAPTER QUESTIONS

CHAPTER TEN

1. Discuss Acts 2:42, reflecting on the four main activities in believers' meetings.
2. What is the New Testament model of giving?
3. Is Jerusalem the best model for church growth today? Why or why not?
4. How do we remove or reduce the cultural barriers and minister the Gospel of Christ to all people?
5. Once we have initially made contact with and ministered to an outcast or gang member, what are some ways to keep them open and wanting to receive the Gospel?

Chapter Eleven

The Widow's Way: Crisis Two

In the Book of Acts (chapter 6), the drama of women who were Hellenistic Jews unfolds. These women were probably Jewish proselytes of Greek heritage who were being unfairly treated in the distribution of food. The Hebrew women were apparently receiving full rations, while the Hellenistic Jews were given the leftovers.

This problem, a legitimate complaint, came to the attention of the apostles, who were fully responsible for all the affairs of the Church. It is estimated that the Church had grown to approximately 35,000 members by the 6th chapter of Acts.

Using the wisdom of God, the apostles made a quality decision. They selected seven men of good report, full of the Holy Ghost and faith. All seven of them were also Hellenistic Jews. In other words, they chose Hellenistic Jews to oversee the Hellenistic Jewish women, making sure their needs were cared for and met. Those that were part of the problem had to solve the problem, a good principle for the modern Church.[7]

If we find a problem in a local church, then the people connected to the problem should be responsible for finding a solution. This is great wisdom.

It is important to note that the first leaders chosen in the church in Jerusalem were deacons, not elders, prophets, apostles, pastors, evangelists or teachers. What the Church

---

[7] Bishop Paul E. Paino, Calvary Ministries International conducts an outstanding teaching in this area. I am indebted to him for his gracious input.

needed first were servants.[8] Of them, Stephen distinguished himself above the rest. Philip eventually became an evangelist and ultimately an apostle, but Stephen was the most powerful in the group. When he was confronted by the leadership of the political forces in Israel, they saw the glory of God upon him. They gnashed their teeth and had him killed. More on the life of Stephen will be presented later in this chapter.

At the time of the "Hellenistic Problem," the Church was estimated to be between four and seven years old. The apostles, with one exception, had followed the pattern transmitted by Christ. They taught, trained, broke bread, prayed, preached the Kingdom, healed the sick and raised the dead.

The Church was alive, vibrant, powerful...and heading for disaster!

Though they had a powerful beginning, their time of troubles would come. Could it be that the plan of God was being constrained by the worldview of the apostles? Sometimes Sauls are needed to move the Church to the fulfillment of God's mandate.

In Acts chapter 8:1 it says,

"Now, Saul who was there, (he was a religious leader at the time) *was in hearty agreement with putting him to death. On that day a great persecution arose against the church in Jerusalem.*

---

[8] Dr. Wagner so clearly explains that these were not ordinary deacons. The fact is, all of them were very powerful men of God who could easily be seen as apostles to the Hellenistic Jews. Dr. Wagner indicates that this was the first church split of sorts. My view is slightly different. I believe every servant of God should also be filled powerfully with the Holy Spirit and be trained and prepared to step into areas of leadership as the Lord opens doors. I do not deny that these were exceptional leaders in this day and time. But the fact is, the priority of the apostles was not to raise up more apostles as much as it was to find servants who understood the heart, purpose and vision of God and were willing to step into an area of great difficulty and assist as God gave them grace to do so.

They were all scattered throughout the regions of Judaea and Samaria except the apostles."

Looking back, what was the mandate that Jesus gave?

His Great Commission was to go into all the world to preach the Gospel.

Who did He give the mandate to?

The eleven. The mandate was received by them, and no doubt was clearly understood. However, their understanding was in light of their cultural context.

What was their orientation context in regards to the Gospel?

They were all Jews. They were raised in Jewish tradition. Their understanding of the Gospel was that it was by the Jews (which is true) and for the Jews, which is true, but not totally. That was their cultural paradigm. Even though Jesus said it was for all nations, their worldview limited their mission (it can limit ours as well!).

Perhaps, they concluded, "All nations that have Jewish believers in them are the ones for which we are responsible." It made perfect sense to establish their mission in their beloved Jerusalem. The Church had to start somewhere, and Jerusalem was the place. However, Jerusalem only was never the plan of God! In their defense, the apostles may not have had a full understanding of the revelation of Jesus. Revelation for us is often progressive, as we are able to receive and understand.

Nonetheless, they had an incredible revival amongst their own people. Culturally, the Jews did not believe themselves responsible for other people groups — not the Samaritans, Romans or Greeks. Their belief seems to have been that if someone else happens to get saved, wonderful. But, they must become Jews first, then they can become Christians. This was a common mind-set of the time.

This belief was powerfully refuted by the Apostle Paul many years later, but the attitude was held by the Jews, and repeated in some present day religious groups. It is anathema to the Kingdom of God! The comfort of a mono-cultural Church had to be disabled. God used the young man Stephen to expand the Kingdom beyond Jerusalem.

Stephen was a unique man of God, full of fire, bold as a lion. Stephen's life was sown for the Gospel; through his death a revival fire was sparked throughout the rest of the world. Stephen's life is seen by some as tragic. But, he was a powerful man of God, full of faith and power. Signs, wonders and miracles abounded though his life until his death. Stephen's life was used to convict the great Apostle Paul to his roots. It is guaranteed; he could never get Stephen out of his mind. Paul must have thought, "Why would a good Jewish boy like Stephen be so stupid as to follow this Jesus? My goodness, doesn't he understand!" Only when he was knocked on his rear, on the road to Damascus, could Paul finally recognize and deal with the Stephen that Jesus stood for, who was shown the majestic glory of God.

Again, the scripture states, *"That everyone was scattered, except the apostles."* It was to the apostles that the commission to go was given. They are the ones that stayed rather than go. This gives credence to the understanding that Jerusalem is not the best model for the development of church life. Many say they want a New Testament church. Many desire to see a Pentecost experience in their church. Unknowingly, they are hoping for a Jerusalem type of church. They would prefer a church filled with people similar to them. Yes, they want the power of the Holy Spirit, to have a sense of Christian community. Yes, they want favor, but do not want persecution. Persecution will likely occur to any group that becomes incestuous, even if it contains a revelation of truth. The scattering that occurred was used to accomplish the mandate of Christ.

It was not God's perfect will to cause a scattering. His desire was to fulfill the mandate of world evangelism, as commissioned to His apostles from the beginning. But they were not able to do so. They were constricted by their cultural context, by their own mental perceptual grid. They were Jews. Jews belong in Jerusalem. They had thousands of people gathering around them. They were conditioned to not accept responsibility for anyone outside of Judaism, or their cultural comfort zone.

Too often we see the same pattern in modern churches. God's people gather together, usually in response to the preaching of the Word and a move of the Holy Spirit. As they gather, there is a certain amount of excitement, as is often the case with any new beginning. Most believers want to receive the blessings of community life, to include the prosperity that comes from following the patterns and purposes of God. However, it is most difficult for people to leave their normal comfort zone, to reach out into communities that are divergent from their own. Even those as close as across the street can be a people with whom it is difficult to link arms. It is a sad commentary on the Church today that so often minor issues separate believers from one another. Though they are all saved and filled with the same precious Holy Spirit, because of a lack of commonality in dress, talk or various cultural customs, they are unable to relate objectively and in love with one another.

This was never God's intention!

God's plan was to release the Good News of the Kingdom of God to the entire world until all the nations are discipled into Christ.

In spite of the apostles' apparent lack of follow through on the Great Commission, the message of Christ continued to spread through the persecution caused by the death of Stephen. It is important to note, however, that the apostles still remained in Jerusalem. So, who did go out from Jerusalem to share the Good News of the risen Messiah?

It was those who had been converted, most likely during the first four years or so in the church in Jerusalem. They were the believers who were taught in houses and on Solomon's porch. They met for the teaching provided by the apostles, times of fellowship, the breaking of bread, communion and prayer. The favor of God was upon them in Jerusalem until the outbreak of persecution.

The early Jerusalem converts sat under the anointed teaching of apostles who were foundation builders, able to impart the gifts of God into others. They had enjoyed this dynamic teaching for almost four years. When Stephen was martyred, the Church scattered. Some went underground. They were most likely Jews that had no other place to go. Those that had a place to flee to ran for their lives. They were primarily lay people, none known to be deacons, let alone elders. They were common disciples that had been trained apostolically in the church of the city in Jerusalem.

When the converts were scattered, things began to happen. The Gospel was preached everywhere! Acts 11:19-26 describes the scene:

> *"So then those who were scattered because of the persecution that arose in connection with Stephen, made their way to Phoenicia, Cyprus and Antioch speaking the word to no one except the Jews alone."*

Why did they speak to Jews alone?

Because that's the way they were discipled. As a sect of Judaism, the "way" was for the Jews. Jesus Himself said to preach to the Jews first. Perhaps the apostles thought, "Until every Jew has heard, we need not preach to Gentiles." Some may have hoped they would never run out of Jews to receive their preaching. This was the unfortunate mind-set of the day.

It is frequently the mind-set of our times as well.

The Widow's Way: Crisis Two

End of Chapter Questions

Chapter Eleven

1. What sociological factors account for the miraculous growth of the church in Jerusalem?
2. What prepared Stephen for his unique role in the expansion of the Church?
3. Describe the dynamics of the Jerusalem model church?

CHAPTER TWELVE

THE BARNABAS BLESSING - THE ANTIOCH PATTERN

The scattering produced a new wave of evangelism. Believers who were trained in Jerusalem naturally shared with friends and neighbors the wonderful grace of God. No one, especially the Jewish apostles in Jerusalem, anticipated what was about to occur as the emphasis of church growth shifted to Antioch.

> "There were some of them, men of Cyprus and Cyrene, who came to Antioch that began speaking to the Greeks also. Preaching the Lord Jesus. And the hand of the Lord was with them."

It is important to note that when believers are doing the perfect will of God, reaching out to their neighbors evangelistically in the love of the Lord, that God's good hand will be upon them. When God's grace is evident, so too will be the results. This includes new converts to Christ, churches being established, and the needs of God's people being met.

The group scattered from Jerusalem because persecution continued to flow in the perfect will of God.

> "A large number who believed, turned to the Lord. And the news about them reached the ears of the church at Jerusalem. And they sent Barnabas off to Antioch. When he had come and witnessed the grace of God, he rejoiced and began to encourage them all with resolute heart to remain true to the Lord."

For approximately one year, Barnabas stayed in Antioch, ministering to the converts there. *"For he was a good man and full of the Holy Spirit in the faith and considerable numbers were brought to the Lord after he was there."* Considerably more people came to the Lord as the work continued to grow, primarily through the teaching ministry of Barnabas, and the help of lay leaders who took the Gospel to Antioch. Most of the new leaders had come from Jerusalem. It was primarily a lay evangelism outreach without a program.

Believers entered the marketplace, sharing Christ wherever they could. They spoke of Christ's life, death and resurrection. Many came to know the Lord through their witness. When these new people professed the Lord, they were automatically enrolled into the school of Barnabas.

Under Christ's authority, Barnabas functioned as a teacher, eventually emerging as an apostle, imparting his gift to all who were being saved. What did he teach them during his leadership? Everything the apostles had taught him during his tutelage in Jerusalem. Barnabas was an interesting fellow, a Hellenistic Jew. He would have been fluent in Greek and familiar with Greek philosophy. He also knew Hebrew, making him a perfect candidate to check out what was happening in Antioch.

Can you imagine what would have happened if James had been sent to Antioch to analyze the movement of God? What a different culture they would have found. The Greeks were highly expressive, emotional, even sensual. Their consummate lifestyle was filled with idol worship, polytheism, sensuality and temple prostitution. This was the "normal lifestyle" of the Greeks of the day. When they were saved, they continued to express themselves according to the basic cultural traits they had prior to their Christian walk.

One could imagine that when they sang a song they did so in a different style than the Jews. When the Jews sang a hymn, they were respectful, even solemn. They did not dance much except at weddings or parties. But the Greeks would have sung very expressively! We might contrast the style of worship at a liturgical church with a Pentecostal or Charismatic one. One is not better than the other, only different. However, since the Church had been started as a

Jewish experience, it was only natural to bring Jewish tradition to bear on the Greeks.

This would have been a total mistake.

The Hebrews understood tradition. Tradition meant everything. How one entered the temple, what one wore, how one spoke was all regulated from birth. Not so with the Greeks. Little was regulated. People got married to get divorced. They got divorced to get married. Everything was very Southern California casual. It was wild. Out of control. Certain adaptations to culture were necessary, without compromise to the Gospel, to reach this new community for Christ.

About Antioch

At one time, Antioch was the third largest city in the Empire, after Alexandria and Rome. It was situated from Antioch westward, through Tarsus (the birthplace of St. Paul), the Cilician Gates, and over a narrow road which provided the only way into the interior of Turkey. The Roman Highway led all the way to Italy.

Its inhabitants were a mixture of all the people of the Empire - Greeks, Persians, Romans, Jews, Syrians and even Russians, or Scythians as they were then called.

Antioch was in the best watered, most fertile part of Turkey.

When Barnabas arrived in the city of Antioch, he came with an understanding of both Hebrew and Greek worldviews. Neither Peter nor James would have had a clear understanding of a Greek mindset, let alone how to integrate a Christian experience into a Greek worldview. Unfortunately, the apostles from Jerusalem most likely would have interpreted what they saw in Antioch according to their own religious paradigm. Their first thought may have been to "let the circumcisions begin," a most unpleasant thought for a Greek male. Further, they may have placed the Greeks into a religious box that would have constrained the move of God, which would have constrained the expansion of the Gospel to the Gentile world.

Barnabas had the ability to understand both worlds. He could relate the Gospel without compromise, teaching the principles of the Word of God while allowing the Holy Spirit to do the work of sanctification in the hearts and lives of the citizenry of Antioch. Who knows what would have happened without the ministry of Barnabas?

Thank God Barnabas was sent. The scriptures describe Barnabas as a man who was full of the Holy Spirit and full of faith. In many ways, he is one of the most important characters of the New Testament in that he was able to bridge the gap from a mono-cultural Christian worldview to at least a bi-cultural focus. Barnabas was able to cross the cultural boundaries, bringing the Gospel to the Gentiles.

Continuing with the scripture, it says,

"He left for Tarsus to look for Saul. When he found him, he brought him to Antioch and it came about that for an entire year they met with the church and taught considerable numbers and the disciples where first called Christians in Antioch."

In Antioch, Barnabas was ministering powerfully, experiencing tremendous success in the Lord. Things were happening; people were growing; God was blessing. The work load must have been extremely difficult. The amount of teaching to be done would be more than one man (no matter how anointed) could bear.

Saul (Paul) must have made an impact on Barnabas. Having met him in Jerusalem (Acts), Saul's vision left an impression upon him. Here was a man who had a call to the Gentiles. Since this was the audience that Barnabas was primarily ministering to, when he needed a partner, Saul was the most logical choice. So, when it came time to look for a helper, Barnabas, realizing that little help would likely come from Jerusalem, went searching for Saul.

Why would he not ask one of the apostles? They would likely have come with their brand of Christianity. Christianity in Jerusalem was more than Judaism, it was a new sect of the covenant of God embracing Jesus as Messiah. In fact, Barnabas probably knew that there was no one qualified for a team ministry concept being established in Antioch. Somehow the Holy Spirit must have spoken to him and reminded him that Saul was called for the divine purpose of reaching the Gentiles.

Saul had been miraculously born-again on the road to Damascus. He spent a significant period of time in personal study with the Lord, receiving direct revelation from Jesus. He spent some time in Jerusalem, but was shunned by the suspicious church. Significant fear surrounded Saul, with concern for Saul's intentions because of his past reputation. Most wondered, "Is he a spy for the Hebrew religion, waiting to attack the Church at some other time?"

The gift of suspicion reigned supreme.

In spite of the lack of a full vision of God's ultimate plan, we must not denigrate the Jewish early church. Jesus was and is the Jewish Messiah. The Church of today should be forever grateful for the Jewish roots of Christianity. The covenant of Abraham was offered to the Gentile as part and parcel of the plan of God. Thus, we are grafted into Abraham's covenant as God's children. As Paul later stated, if the grafted (Gentiles) are valuable, how much more the original (Jews) branches. Without a thorough understanding of the Jewishness of our Christian heritage in God's Word, and the debt owed to our Hebrew brethren, we would make worse mistakes than did the apostles in Jerusalem.

Barnabas, though he was most likely in the midst of a wonderful time of teaching and ministering in Antioch, recognized his need for assistance and went to Tarsus to find Saul. When he found him, Saul was most likely involved in his vocational pursuit: tent making. There is no indication that Saul (Paul) was active in ministry of any type. It had been several years since the Church had been established on the day of Pentecost. It had been several years since Stephen's death. Yet Saul (Paul), the great man of God, had essentially been on the back burner, on the back side of a desert, traversing through his wilderness experience prior to his release into active ministry.

When Barnabas arrived in Tarsus, I assume Saul was greatly relieved. Very likely he was packed and ready to go. He had been waiting for years for the opportunity to enter full-time ministry, to fulfill the vision the Lord had given him on the road to Damascus. He returned with Barnabas to Antioch, where the native people would not have known of Saul's dubious reputation. If Barnabas told them that Saul was a necessary part of the team, a great man of God, anointed, called as an apostle, that was sufficient.

What a blessing Saul must have been to the new converts in Antioch. The disciples in Antioch easily accepted the apostle Paul because of his unique anointing, and because Barnabas provided covering for him. "If Barnabas said he is okay, he must be okay."

When they arrived, they taught together for a period of one year, as a dynamic team raising up disciples. Through this teaching process, the believers were first called "Christians." Their teaching brought the life of Christ to the service of these new believers — "little Christs."

They had a very powerful teaching ministry. Barnabas was the lead teacher, and Saul his associate, amongst others who were actively discipling the believers. Since Saul had been rejected by the church in Jerusalem, he still needed to learn the dynamics of church life. As an associate of Barnabas, he would wait patiently, taught faithfully, recognizing that the gift of God was also on Barnabas and not just on him. Saul did his internship under Barnabas. It was later, of course, that Paul became the lead teacher and Barnabas, the associate; probably a more comfortable role for both.

Acts 11:27 says, *"Now at this time some prophets came down from Jerusalem to Antioch."*

Where did the prophets come from? They emerged through the teaching ministry, under apostolic authority, in the church in Jerusalem. It has always been God's plan to raise up the ministry gifts from within the body, the church in locality. The prophets came to deliver a message of great importance. A famine was coming, which would have had devastating results. The church in Antioch took a special offering for the Jerusalem church, sending it back with their two leaders to Jerusalem. This was the first return for Barnabas to Jerusalem. He avoided reporting back to Jerusalem, demonstrating God's favor and Barnabas' wisdom. His pastoral heart would not allow the grace of God to be bound by the Judaisers of Jerusalem.

A determination was made by the leadership of the church in Antioch to send Barnabas and Saul. As mentioned previously, the order of these two men, in terms of how they are listed in scripture, is of great significance. Barnabas was clearly the lead in Antioch. Later, after the Holy Spirit sent them out from Antioch to plant churches in the Gentile world, Saul became preeminent in ministry and leadership. As the scriptures indicate, Saul was called directly by the Lord Himself; Barnabas was not...yet. Since Saul had not fully experienced church life, he was not qualified to assume the fullness of a leadership position within local church ministry. Even with the apostle Paul, a most gifted man of God, there was a time and season of preparation before release, all to be done in the sovereignty of God.

This same dynamic still occurs in local churches around the world. Often the senior pastor is a less gifted preacher than the young men and women under his or her charge. And yet, it is vitally important that a potential minister remain under the pastor's charge for a time of preparation. This allows the transference of all the knowledge the senior minister has gained through his service in the Body of Christ and allows sufficient time to mentor young leaders into fuller maturity.

Saul needed time and opportunity to experience the Church. The Saints in Jerusalem had rejected him out of fear, so he learned church life in other places. God provided for his nurturing in Antioch, as well as for the blossoming of his gifts and call for the future.

The church in Antioch was a dynamic, powerful church. God's grace abounded. In the church at Antioch, a revised model for the expansion of the Kingdom of God is found. This is most clearly presented in the 13th chapter of the book of Acts. In this chapter Barnabas, Saul and the Church take another step in their journey, building the type of Church God really desires. Here is the beginning of the five-fold ministry in action, in support of the development of the local church, and the sending forth of apostolic teams for church planting.

Chapter 13:1-4 says;

"Now there were at Antioch in the church that was there. There were prophets and teachers, Barnabas and Simeon who was called Niger. Lucius of Cyrene, and Manaen, who had been brought up with Herod, the tetrarch, and Saul. While they were ministering to the Lord and fasting, the Holy Spirit said, 'Set apart for me, Barnabas and Saul. For the work which I have called them to.' Then when they had fasted and prayed and laid their hands on them, they sent them away, so being sent..."

There is no indication from this passage that the men and women found in the city of Antioch were any more special, dynamic or gifted than in Jerusalem. In fact, they had many disadvantages, especially as one compares them to the church in Jerusalem. And yet, God used this powerful church to begin the process of discipling the nations of the known world with the Gospel. Who were these converts in Antioch? They had been won to Christ by the believers and scattered due to the persecution in Jerusalem. These godly men and women were used by God in Antioch, raised up to greater leadership through the teaching ministry of Barnabas and Saul.

Another essential point to consider is that prophets and teachers emerged in the city of Antioch. This means that Barnabas and Saul were considered both prophets and teachers, but they were not yet apostles. Their apostleship did not occur until the Holy Spirit spoke, releasing them into greater responsibility and authority. Once designated, through the anointing of the Holy Spirit, to be apostles, or ones sent out for the purpose of planting churches and expanding the Kingdom of God, the expansion of the Church began. Further, there were other teachers, prophets, etc., which God raised up within the city of Antioch through the teaching, apostolic ministry presented by Barnabas and later, Saul.

In our modern era, the closest thing found to true apostolic ministry would be missionaries sent out by the Holy Spirit to various nations to plant churches and establish ministries, as well as men and women of God who are foundation builders, church planters within a local community. Apostles are active in church planting, in building up the saints, in equipping God's people and releasing them into greater areas of service. Apostles are called by Christ and sent to do a specific purpose, of a foundational nature. This area of ministry is being restored to the Church and remains a vital area of ministry for the 21st Century.

Before Barnabas and Saul became apostles, they first had to prove themselves faithful in other areas of ministry or service. They were teachers and prophets serving God's people within the local fellowship. As previously mentioned, Barnabas had not even been designated a deacon before coming to Antioch! Through the dynamic processes of the Holy Spirit, as they taught faithfully the Word of God, giving to others, blessing and ministering to the saints, God, in a very unique and special way matured Paul and Barnabas until they were released into greater service. The Holy Spirit prepared them for greater levels of ministry, and when it was time, released them into their apostolic call.

This is the precise pattern God intends for the local church today. Through training, teaching, discipleship and relationship, God begins to empower by the Holy Spirit individuals in preparation for greater service.

After the disciples were trained, and the transformation of character accomplished (first called Christians), the Holy Spirit spoke. How God spoke, we are not told. It was probably not an audible voice, but, as they were praying and fasting, the awareness of the plan of God became clear. Perhaps God spoke by prophetic word. In other words, a normal part of their spiritual life was to have times of specific, concentrated prayer and fasting. Daily devotions and times of teaching were consistently conducted. But this was a special time of prayer and fasting. During one of these meetings, the Holy Spirit spoke to the collective body and they had ears to hear, sensitized by continual communion with the Holy Spirit.

A question has often crossed my mind. Why would God take the cream-of-the-crop out of this church and send them to the mission field? God chose the leaders of this fellowship and sent them to another place to start a new adventure — the expansion of the Kingdom. Why would God not have chosen someone with a good gifting, a nice calling, good looking, nice bank account, to send out to plant churches, to return under Barnabas and Saul's authority?

The only logical assumption is that the Holy Spirit knew what He was doing. Christ is the head of the Church. My guess is that there was sufficient leadership in the local church, people well trained and able to emerge to the place of leadership vacated by Barnabas and Saul. Thus, after they prayed and fasted, they were sent out. There were others in the church, prepared under the teaching ministry, who stepped into the role of greater leadership. They had been prepared for such a time as this.

This is the natural progression of spiritual things. God sends someone out to allow someone else to step into a place of service and leadership. Of course, this is not always the case. Many times, others under a pastor's authority will be sent out apostolically. Clearly, this is part of the ministry of the Holy Spirit to prepare people within the local church through the teaching ministry, so that in time and season they can be brought into the fullness of their position in God, and released into ministry.

How dynamic, yet systematic is the plan of God.

THE PROCESS OF RELEASE

Notice the priority of ministry.

First, they ministered to the Lord, most likely through prayer and worship. Verse two says, *"And while they were ministering to the Lord and fasting."* The priority of ministry was not preaching, teaching, or even evangelism. In the ministry, all are called to minister to the Lord. This was a dynamic part of the church in Antioch. The leadership must have consistently modeled the importance of a lifestyle of worship, to the Lord first.

Second, they would minister to others. Thus, they could minister to others out of the abundant flow of the Holy Spirit, not from worn-out flesh.

Third, they fasted and prayed to center their focus purely upon what God would say or do. Prayer with fasting allows us to maintain our spiritual equilibrium. It allows the flow of God's Word and purpose into our hearts. Fasting provides time where we can set ourselves aside to receive specifically from the Lord and freshen our focus on Him.

Praise and worship provided the spiritual power to receive from God while they fasted and prayed. This should cause every believer to realize the importance of our lifestyle of worship. It was then that the Holy Spirit spoke.

In an atmosphere of praise and worship, the elders laid hands on Barnabas and Saul to transfer God's blessing and confirm what God had spoken. Often leaders lay hands on people to call something forth, rather than just confirming what God has already spoken. This could be why Paul later told Timothy not to lay hands on someone quickly, but wait until their character and call were tested through life experience. He was to test them, to make sure they had a true call and maturity to fulfill their call. It must be determined that they are ready before pouring a blessing upon them, transferring the authority to minister in a greater calling.

Part of this daily church ceremony was the transferring of the authority for greater ministry. Jesus transferred His authority. The apostles transferred theirs. It was done in the timing of God. Once someone had been fully prepared, hands were laid on them, transferring God's blessing, confirming the Word of the Lord that had been spoken.

Then they were sent out.

The cream-of-the-crop; the best were sent for God's greater purpose.

A Training Model

What happens in modern-day churches? How does our pattern compare to the 1st Century Church models? An example might help.

A certain pastor has a young man or woman in their congregation who becomes born-again at twelve or thirteen years of age. Shortly thereafter, the young person senses a call of God for service upon their life. Initially, they will talk to their pastor, sharing their desire to prepare for ministry. Most pastors will advise, "That's great! Let me start getting some Bible College catalogs to you. If you work real hard in high school, perhaps you can go to the Bible College where I went. It was good enough for me and it will be good enough for you."

Usually, if the young person can last until they are eighteen, and if they still have a zeal for God, they may very well go off to the Bible College that the pastor attended. This college, most likely an outstanding institution, is usually not in the same city as the church, even in the same state. The faithful student will go away to college and sit under the teaching of many professors. Some of these men or women may be very anointed, called specifically to the teaching ministry.

Unfortunately, this is a rarity.

In most cases the professors are teaching the dead letter. In fact, it is a generalization that if one fails in pastoral ministry they become a Bible teacher. Many Bible Colleges in America have sincere men and women who are teaching with little enthusiasm or impartation.

Typically, what is transferred to a student attending a normal Bible College program is the ability to be a Bible College teacher. This is only natural. To understand the Word of God and to be able to present it in an expository or topical fashion to a group of people in a lecture format is what is taught. Why does this occur? Because professors have learned to teach the same way in their Bible Colleges. They have received the anointing or the transference of that style of ministry, exactly as they experienced from their professors.

After 3-4 years (or more) of college and seminary, if the student returns to the local church, they usually carry a conviction that they now know more than the local pastor. In colleges, they have learned all the latest church growth strategies. They are versed in the latest homiletic style. Thus, they tend towards an unteachable attitude if they ever do return (less than one percent ever return to their local church). Even if the local church paid to send them, which they often do, most will never return labor to the land in the church which sent them. Though they may not be lost to the Kingdom of God, the investment of the local church and its leaders is often lost.

If a student returns, it will take an average of two years before they are able to flow in the vision of that local church. The church has continued to function while the student was away at college. The church has not stopped its vision, programs or outreach. Naturally, the church has matured, moving in different directions as seen as necessary by the leadership. Fitting back into that model can be most difficult.

What is the problem with this model of discipleship development?

For the most part, it is an ill-conceived adaptation to culture. The Christian community has strayed far from the biblical pattern. The majority of churches are doing all they know to reach their community for Christ, given the models they experienced for training. That is, many local churches focus on spiritual events and activities to entertain the consumer-oriented Christian market.

It takes time to move an entire group of people in a specific direction. It's much easier to change people one person at a time. When we're talking about change and growth in the local church, we're talking about attempting to produce change in people who have an internalized, preconceived concept of what church life involves. Changing these notions is a very difficult task. Sending people away from the local church will not bring change. For true change, leaders must provide purposeful, visionary teaching within the church of the locality.

Much of our difficulty comes because our model for education and training has been removed from the laboratory that God created for ministry development. That laboratory is the local church, or the church in the locality. It is in the book of Acts that this model is found. The cream-of-the-crop was never lost to the church at Antioch. They were trained and educated within the local community; sent out to duplicate itself again. This is the primary biblical model for ministry expansion, an apostolic/prophetic paradigm, which is slowly re-emerging in the modern Church.

MUTUAL ACCOUNTABILITY

In chapter 14 of the Book of Acts, Paul and Barnabas returned to Antioch and maintained a relational covenant with that local assembly. Notice in chapter 14, when Paul and Barnabas returned to the local church, they sat with the elders. They did not return to rule over them. They returned to join the community of faith to which they were responsible. They were unconcerned about positional power, but focused on building the church according to pattern.

This pattern of mutual accountability is one of grave importance for the Church today. In the church at Antioch, the people that sent out Barnabas and Saul, later Paul and Barnabas, had a deep personal relationship with them. It was a vigorous relationship based upon mutual respect, love and covenant. While Paul and Barnabas were away in ministry, no doubt the disciples in Antioch kept them at the top of their prayer list. When they sent them out, they did so with their blessing, but also with the necessary financial resources to carry out their work for the Lord. As such, Paul and Barnabas had a conventional responsibility to report back to the church in Antioch regarding the activities of their ministry.

I am certain that while they were gone, the church at Antioch was on the apostles' hearts. They would have prayed for that church, groaning before the Lord, trusting God to protect the sheep that had been established within that city. When they returned to Antioch, they did so with great joy. They did not return as the great apostles to pontificate all that they had learned, though they would have been deferred to by the elders within the city. Paul and Barnabas understood that the church had continued to progress during their absence. As such, they would not have returned to lord over it or give absolute direction to that local assembly, but would have joyfully sat with them, fellowshipped with them, and contributed to them from all that God had done during their missionary ventures.

This mutual giving and receiving, loving and caring for one another with mutual accountability is part of the pattern that is desperately needed within church life today. It is so unfortunate that many local fellowships do not even know the missionaries they financially support. They may hear from them once every four years when it's time for them to up their financial commitment. This is a long way from the New Testament pattern. Those doing the sending knew those to be sent. They had a mutually accountable relationship, which was a blessing to all involved. This relationship provided safety, prayer support, financial blessing and resulted in the growth of the Kingdom of God.

End of Chapter Questions

Chapter Twelve

1. Describe some of the dynamics of the church in Antioch. How were they different from Jerusalem?
2. What problems might have occurred if James had been sent to Antioch rather than Barnabus? Can you make modern applications?
3. Why was Saul/Paul so important to the ministry at Antioch?
4. How is the model of ministry training and the releasing of ministries today different from Antioch? Elaborate.

Chapter Thirteen

The Ephesus Model

Paul, in his traveling ministry, found some converts who were won to the Lord by the Apostle Apollos in the city of Ephesus. This is discussed in the 19th chapter of the book of Acts. A continuing picture of the dynamics for church growth and development can be seen in the ministry of the Apostle Paul to this small group of converts.

"And it came about that while Apollos was at Corinth, Paul having passed through the upper country came to Ephesus, and found some disciples, and he said to them, 'Did you receive the Holy Spirit when you believed?' And they said to him, 'No, we have not even heard whether there is a Holy Spirit.' And he said, 'Into what then were you baptized?' And they said, 'Into John's baptism.' And Paul said, 'John baptized with the baptism of repentance, telling the people to believe in Him who was coming after him, that is, in Jesus.' And when they heard this, they were baptized in the name of the Lord Jesus. And when Paul had laid his hands upon them, the Holy Spirit came on them, and they began speaking with tongues and prophesying. And there were in all about twelve men. And he entered the synagogue and continued speaking out boldly for three months, reasoning and persuading them about the Kingdom of God. But when some were becoming hardened and disobedient, speaking evil of the way before the multitude, he withdrew from them and took away the disciples, reasoning daily in the school of Tyrannus. And this took place for two years, so that all who lived in Asia heard the word of the Lord, both Jews and Greeks," (Acts 19:1-10, NASB).

Let's look at what occurred through the ministry of the Apostle Paul in the city of Ephesus.

As is true in apostolic ministry, the Apostle Paul was concerned about the foundations of the lives of the converts he found. As was true in the ministry of Jesus, Paul interviewed those that he encountered. He handled first things first, asking them about their salvation experience. What an important question to ask any new convert encountered within a local fellowship. "Tell us about your salvation experience?" should be a primary question. I have run across many situations in my ministry where people in leadership (usually not the pastor) never actually had a "born-again" experience.

How tragic.

Paul was not going to make the mistake of not asking. He did not assume anything. He looked for first things first. Then he talked to them about the Holy Spirit in their lives. When they answered with honesty that they did not even know who the Holy Spirit was, Paul got down to business. He baptized them in water, identifying them with the death, burial and resurrection of Christ and fully identifying them with the Church of Jesus Christ. As they emerged from the waters of baptism, Paul laid hands on them and they were baptized in the Holy Spirit, evidenced by speaking in tongues and prophecy. Please note that they did not have to attend school or go through classes to be trained to speak in tongues or prophesy. This is part of the apostolic ministry, the impartation of the gift of the Holy Spirit to individuals who are open to receive.

Following this, the Apostle Paul began teaching them the principles of Christian living. They attended synagogue together. He taught everyone that came, but with a primary focus on the twelve disciples and the many others that would soon join him because of his persuasive preaching of the Gospel.

What were the results of His teaching?

The Ephesus Model

What is the model that the Apostle Paul is expanding in Ephesus?

The apostle, *"Continued speaking out boldly for three months. Reasoning and persuading them about the Kingdom of God."* He didn't preach on his favorite topics, he preached the Kingdom! The results were health, prosperity and God's blessing. The admonition of Christ in Matthew 6:33 was, *"Seek ye first the Kingdom of God and his righteousness and all of these things will be added unto you."* That is to be the focus of all ministries, to keep things in proper priority. They did not preach to build the Church. They preached the Kingdom, and the Church emerged.

The scripture continues,

"When some were becoming hardened and disobedient, speaking evil of the way, before the multitude, he withdrew from them and took away the disciples, reasoning daily in the school of Tyrannus."

Most likely, the school of Tyrannus was a rented school hall. This school may have been a center for the training of Jewish or Hellenistic Jewish believers, or a children's school. Whether or not Tyrannus was a Christian we do not know. We do not even know if he was alive at the time; they may have named the school after him. In either case, Paul purposefully gathered the believers to himself.

Notice it says, *"And this took place for two years."* Paul began teaching disciples daily, ministering to them. Certain ones received the Lord and were attentive to Paul's teaching. Then there arose opposition. When the opposition came, rather than fighting, Paul simply moved to another building in another area where he could continue to teach and disciple these men and women of God.

What did Paul teach?

Everything Barnabas taught, which was everything the apostles taught, which was everything Jesus taught. It's called the apostles' doctrine. Further, they probably broke bread, prayed and fellowshipped, house-to-house, because this was the model previously learned. These were not merely social activities. When it was time to pray, they all prayed.

Verse 10 says, *"And this took place for two years so that all who lived in Asia heard the word of the Lord, both Jews and Greeks."* Who did they hear the Gospel through? From the disciples being trained under the ministry of Paul. Then, in verse eleven: *"And God was performing extraordinary miracles by the hands of Paul."* Extraordinary miracles occurred after the time of teaching.

First teaching, then miracles...just as in Jesus' ministry.

Jesus went about teaching, casting out demons, and healing all who were oppressed of the devil; so did the apostles. This was and still should be a primary ministry of the Church of Jesus Christ. This pattern flowed through the apostolic and prophetic ministry, primarily a foundation of faith in Christ, repentance from dead works, etc., as seen in Hebrews chapter 6. This continued until disciples were mature enough to spread the Gospel, ministering in the format of the Apostle Paul. The long-term goal of this ministry was the planting of local churches, indigenous works, culturally sensitive and yet clearly biblical. These churches would provide nurturing and ministry for the next generation.

As Paul taught, leaders were developed. They grew in God according to the gifts of God found in the life of the individual disciple. Ministry would emerge, including deacons and elders, but also, the five-fold ministry. Prophets, evangelists, teachers, pastors, and no doubt, other apostles were raised up through the teaching ministry of Paul and other teachers whom Paul utilized as necessary. These men and women were equipped and restored, raised up within the local fellowship, and in time sent out to do the work of the Lord. Eventually, as the Church matured, and strong leadership was established through the ministry of elders and deacons, the Apostle Paul moved on to his next missionary venue.

Here again, the pattern already well established in Paul's mind and spirit is demonstrated. What pattern was he following? The same pattern seen in the life and ministry of Jesus. The same pattern exhibited through the lives of the Jerusalem apostles. The same pattern that Paul experienced in Antioch under the ministry of Barnabas, his mentor and co-laborer. The disciples Paul taught were equipped in areas of righteousness, had similar desires to know the Word, to practice it and teach it, as Ezra had in the Old Testament. Through the teaching ministry, the Kingdom of God was expanded. A bonus to that teaching ministry was the extraordinary signs, wonders and miracles that began to flow through the ministry of the Apostle Paul, and no doubt occurred through many of his disciples as they followed his pattern of ministry.

The Supernatural

The Apostle Peter had some pretty phenomenal things happen in his ministry. His shadow was enough to cause people to be healed. The miracles through Paul, Peter and other disciples must have been truly exciting as they saw miracles flow in the pattern that God had established.

When a church steps out of the pattern of God, they court certain danger. They will rarely see the desired results. The results of ministry should be the transformation of a community stretching beyond their boundaries. The church in Antioch, and then the church in Ephesus, became great missionary churches of the time, but not the church in Jerusalem. Jerusalem was always the mother church, honored and revered. It was, and always will be seen as the heart of the New Testament Church.

Though we may be most fond of the church in Jerusalem, and grateful for the church developed there, the best model for ministry to the Gentile community must be that of the churches in Antioch and Ephesus. In both of these churches, the model for the development or growth of the Church is established. Each church was founded by a dynamic move of the Holy Spirit through lay leaders who were willing to witness beyond their community. The fields are always ripe for harvest somewhere. It is inherent on church leadership to be led by the Holy Spirit to know where the fields are ripe, so they can have effective evangelistic ministry.

Once new converts are found, they must be built up in the precious faith of the Lord Jesus Christ through teaching, laying a solid foundation for the purposes of God [Apostolic ministry] and the vision that God has [prophetic ministry] for their community. This foundation was built over a period of two years of full-time teaching ministry with Barnabas and Paul, and later Paul and Silas. Timothy and Titus followed a similar pattern because the master teacher, the Apostle Paul, trained them.

The long-term result was a supernatural Church where the gifts of the Holy Spirit were in operation, evangelism was the focus, and church planting was the long-term aim. Those established in leadership, the cream-of-the-crop, were ultimately sent out by the power of the Holy Spirit to develop new ministries as the Lord opened doors.

This is still the model God has for today. It is unfortunate that we see so little of this dynamic in local churches, but much more of that will be discussed in the last section of this book.

The Ephesus Results: A Brief Commentary

The results of the Apostle Paul's ministry in Antioch are discussed some within Church history. However, the letter the Apostle Paul wrote to the church in Ephesus speaks powerfully of the results of his ministry, and the pattern established throughout his ministry in that city. Thus, it is important to review briefly, with comments, this wonderful book, to understand what occurred, and the importance of it within the city of Ephesus.

Though there is some debate as to whether or not Paul was the actual author of the book of Ephesians, most would agree that it is distinctly Pauline in nature. This book is called "The Gospel according to Paul." Found here is Paul's interpretation of the meaning or the purpose of Christ's coming. As with John, the great and beloved apostle, he begins this letter by looking at things eternal from the beginning, rather than from the time of Christ's earthly ministry.

In the first chapter of Ephesians, he starts with:

> *"Paul an apostle of Christ Jesus, by the will of God to the saints who are at Ephesus and who are faithful in Christ Jesus. Grace to you and peace from God our Father and the Lord Jesus Christ. Blessed be the God and Father of our Lord Jesus Christ who has blessed us with every spiritual blessing in the heavenly places in Christ just as he chose us in him, before the foundation of the world."*

God chose the Church from the beginning. It was not an afterthought. The choice God made was for the Church to receive all spiritual blessings in the heavenly places in Christ. All believers are seated in those same heavenly places, yet we are still here on Earth. It's part of our dual citizenship. We are citizens of this world and citizens of heaven with Christ.

Continuing,

> *"Just as he chose us from the foundation of the world, that we should be holy, set aside for his purpose, and blameless before him. In love or because of love, he predestined us to adoption as sons through Jesus Christ to himself. According to the kind, generous, merciful intention of his own will."*

Why did God choose the church in Ephesus? Because He wanted to. It was out of His own kind intention. God's desire was to establish the Church, the Bride of Christ, adorned for His Son. He adopted us all as His children so that we might have a complete and full inheritance, to fulfill a destiny predetermined for us from the beginning of all things.

This is truly an exciting proposition!

A New Testament church is a church that has understood and embraced its destiny. This includes the reality of their calling, the truth that we are, as God's children, adopted into His family, never to be unadopted, chosen by Him to fulfill a great purpose. Paul states a wonderful and profound truth. We have been chosen because God wanted us, loved us and determined from the beginning of time to build His church for His glory.

Verse 6 says,

> *"To the praise of the glory of his grace, which he freely bestowed on us in the beloved, through Christ. In him we have redemption through his blood, the forgiveness of our sins or trespasses, according to the riches of his grace, which he lavished upon us. In all wisdom and insight, he made known to us the mystery of his will."*

The mystery of His will was revealed through the life of Christ: the plan of redemption for all mankind. A major component of that mystery was that the Gentiles, not just the Jews, would be included in salvation, purchased by the blood of Christ. Every nation was to be part of God's marvelous redemptive plan. Each person was to be discipled to maturity by his anointed and appointed apostolic company.

Why did God bring to us that mystery?

Because God is all-wise with total insight into the needs of mankind. He therefore unveiled the mystery of His perfect will by providing His own Son as a sacrifice for many.

If the Church could fully embrace this revelation, what a difference it would make! It is the Father's heart to so infill each believer, and ultimately each church within a locality, with Himself, so each church would become a church without spot or wrinkle, fulfilling their call and destiny. Not only was it His intention to birth the Church, but His intention was to fully administer it, or establish godly government for all nations. This comes through the "summing up" of all things in Christ. A just God has established His perfect government in heaven, so it is His intention to establish godly government, the Kingdom of God on Earth.

God desires to see His Church actively reclaiming all that the devil has stolen in every sphere of life. This includes the political realm, financial strongholds, and the religious community. When we as the children of God come into the fullness of our adopted status and begin to live the way God intended in and through His Church, the Kingdom of God will be expanded and the administration of that Kingdom will occur.

The administration, the government of God began through the "Logos", the Living Word, and continues through the Living Word, as administrated by the Holy Spirit and expressed through the Church here on Earth. God has chosen to work through the five-fold ministry, elders, deacons and other gifted men and women to establish His Kingdom, or His government. His purpose is to bring everything back into proper order. Ultimately, when Christ returns, the Kingdom will be presented to Christ, and Christ will present the Kingdom to the Father.

"In him also we have obtained an inheritance having been predestined according to his purpose who works all things after the counsel of his own will. To the end that we who were first to hope in Christ, should be to the praise of his glory. In him you also after listening to the message of the truth, the Gospel of your salvation. Having also believed you were sealed in him with the Holy Spirit of

promise who was given as a pledge of our inheritance."

How wonderful is the knowledge of our inheritance from the Lord! This inheritance was received when we were born-again, filled with the Spirit of God. Through this pledge, the Holy Spirit, we receive an impartation of the divine nature of God, allowing us to become a supernatural people, a royal priesthood and a holy nation (I Peter 2:4-5, 9-10). In truth, through Christ, by the Holy Spirit, we are already all of those things. We are more than conquerors through Christ. Whether we seem to be or not, part of what has been given to us as our inheritance in Christ is His divine nature in place of our old nature.

It is not natural, but supernatural.

It is the gift of God, given to us by Jesus Christ.

The Apostle Paul is merely reminding the church in the city of all the things he had previously taught them. In his letter, he is summarizing the truth that he had previously spoken to them during his teaching ministry in the city of Ephesus. No doubt it was wonderful for them to review, in writing, the essence of Paul's ministry, a review that was helpful to them in their walk in the Lord.

In Verse 14 he continues,

"Who has given us as a pledge of our inheritance with a view to the redemption of God's own procession to the praise of his glory. For this reason, I too, having heard of the faith in the Lord Jesus which exists among you."

The Apostle Paul kept track of the church in Ephesus. After he had been there for two years, God sent him to regions beyond for church development. He sent Timothy to become the overseer of the church of the city. Timothy's reports of the church's activities probably came to Paul on a regular basis. Thus, with specific information, he could focus his prayers to the Lord. Verse 16 and 17 read:

> *"I do not cease giving thanks for you while making mention of you in my prayers that the God of our Lord Jesus Christ, the Father of glory, may give to you a spirit of wisdom and of revelation in the knowledge of Him."*

Paul's prayer life must have been most powerful. The impetus of his prayers seems to have been on the churches that he had been instrumental in founding or developing.

The Apostle Paul understood that Jesus is the founder of the Church, and that He has given to us very clear patterns for the foundation and development of church life. In Paul's prayer, the priority that Father God has for the local church is presented.

What is it that the Father would like to see within the Church in our day and time?

He would want the same things that Paul prays for here. That is, to see the full and complete purpose of God accomplished through the manifestation of a clear revelation of Who Jesus is for the Church. The purpose for the gathering of a local fellowship is expressed in Paul's prayer...to experience Jesus in all of His fullness.

In the Church today, much activity is focused on meeting the consumer needs of those who attend the fellowship. Many people are coming to local churches because they are lonely, looking for a social group in which to belong, or they are experiencing troubles in some aspect of their lives. Certainly, the local church can be that hospital where people's needs are met. Those things are important, and often lead people to a relationship with Christ. But, ultimately, the purpose for the gathering of the church goes far beyond social activities or the meeting of basic human needs.

As we experience Jesus, growing in His Word and developing relationship with one another, the wisdom of God begins to become our own. As we encounter the Lord, we learn to pray, to fellowship, to witness, to worship. In all of these things, we learn to bring glory to God, the One who is deserving of all praise.

As we continue in these activities, our lives become transformed. We are able to move beyond our own limitations, the boundaries that we have set upon ourselves. We begin to experience the fullness of God's intention for our lives. The purpose is so that...

> "The God of our Lord Jesus Christ, the Father of Glory, may give unto you a spirit of wisdom, the revelation and the knowledge of Him. I pray that the eyes of your heart may be enlightened."

The Apostle Paul was concerned about the growth and development of our spirit man so that we would be filled completely with the light of God's Word and His purposes.

He continues.

> "So that you may know what is the hope of his calling and what are the riches of the glory of his inheritance in the saints and what is the surpassing greatness of his power toward us who believe."

What does the Lord want and intend?

That our eyes would be opened, filled with light, that our hearts would be transformed by the power of His Word until we understand the fullness of the hope of His calling.

God has called each individual who is born-again to a specific fellowship for a specific purpose. Of course, a portion of that purpose includes salvation, provided to us by the Lord Jesus Christ. But why, specifically, are we a part of any given fellowship at any given time? Is it merely because we need a sense of family?

We need that, but there is more.

Is it because we need help to overcome problems?

Yes, but so much more.

What is the hope of our calling?

The hope of our calling is that we might fulfill the eternal destiny that God preordained for our lives within the Kingdom of God. That is, that we might become fully functional members of His community of faith called the Church. However, to become a fully functioning member, we must be socialized into the life of the church. This occurs through the training and teaching done within the local church. As we are trained, taught, counseled, encouraged, exhorted, sometimes corrected, we grow in God until we mature in love and service to the Lord and one another.

At least this is the theory.

Unfortunately, the reality is often different. Many believers have been and are socialized into dysfunctional, legalistic, non-committed life patterns, adaptations of our existing culture. Rather than focusing on Christ and spiritual growth, the emphasis is giftings and charismatic activity. Rules are implemented to control behavior, voiding the grace of God. Of course, none of this is new. Legalism and licentiousness have been equally practiced in every church since the time of the apostles.

Oh, how we need a true Apostolic Reformation to set the Church in order!

Paul's prayers center his teaching on eternal values. Paul understood that if one's heart was filled with the light of God's righteousness, peace and joy in the Holy Spirit (Romans 14:17), that our lives would soon follow in the direction God intends. As we are filled, we will be able to give out. As we are changed, we will become change agents for others within our community.

And what will we look like when we are changed?

We will look like God's people.

Like they were in Antioch. Christians filled with the life of Christ, acting as little Christs. Ultimately, we will begin to experience the glory of God, which is what He intended for His Church.

Some in the Body of Christ today have had a taste of the glory of God. Many have had wonderful experiences, especially during this time of heightened spiritual renewal. We can be amazed and dazed by various phenomenon as people are touched by the power of God. But there is so much more that God intends for us than just experiences. He wants us to embrace the fullness of the life of Christ living, breathing in and through us. This occurs through a deeper communion with the Lord than what most have yet to experience.

As Jesus had wonderful, sweet and precious communion with His Father, a truly intimate relationship with Him, so God wants us to have sweet communion and intimate relationship with Him and each other today. Jesus came to show us the Father. Paul's greatest desire was that people would know Jesus. If they knew Him fully, they would know the Father as well. Preachers today should have the same goal for their people — to know Christ fully, not to praise the preacher, but Christ. They, as Moses, wanted to see and experience the glory of God. God reveals His glory when all the goodness, mercy and kindness of God is manifested in the life of an individual believer within a corporate setting.

It is His glory that will be revealed (Ephesians 33:18-19)!

How could Paul give the glory of God to those that he was teaching? This can only occur through impartation. As he shared with the disciples what God had done in his life, as he ministered the Word of God under the anointing of the Holy Spirit, their lives were changed. The teaching of the taught Word produced an inheritance for them, transference of knowledge and wisdom, and also the power of God. This remains God's will. It is vital that the apostles and prophets emerge in ministry and function together as a team to establish a new, fresh foundation for the Church.

There were times when Paul was tired, broken and frustrated, but never in despair. He understood his inheritance. He could abase or abound. Of course, abounding is better. But like Paul, we can live with whatever comes if we know our calling. As we embrace our inheritance and destiny, we are be able to fulfill our purpose in the Lord.

These things were *"according to the working of the strength of his might which he brought out in Christ when he raised him from the dead."* It's not based upon our strength, knowledge or ability.

Whose Church is it, anyway?

It's Jesus' Church! He is going to build it! He chooses who He wants to use in that process. Being filled with the full revelation of Jesus...that is the key to a Supernatural Architecture.

We must strive for it as Paul did.

"When he raised him from the dead and seated him at his right hand in the heavenly places. Far above all rule and authority and power and dominion and every name that is named. Not only in this age but also in the age to come."

Jesus was lifted up because He did His job. He was faithful to His call. Jesus is no longer the light of the world, we are. Jesus is no longer directly, actively building His church, we are (by the direction of the Holy Spirit). Jesus is no longer ministering here on Earth, we are. He is directing it; He's the head. He is sitting. He is done. He has entered His rest. He has poured His blood out on the mercy seat.

It is finished!

The job of Jesus today is to intercede for His Church. His prayers focus on seeing our purpose on Earth fulfilled. If you will, His prayer would be, "Father, keep helping them." It would be such a blessing if we came into agreement with the prayers of Christ to the Father. It is difficult for us to do that if we are continuously looking for self-satisfaction or attempting to determine again, "Does God really love us, and are we truly forgiven?" Our prayers should be centered on the establishment and expansion of the Kingdom of God. If it is, we will not be looking at ourselves, but at others. And when our view is on others, and on the purposes of God, our lives will line up with God's intention for His Church.

"Hath put all things in subjection under his feet and gave him as head over all things to the church which is his body, the fullness of him who fills all in all."

What is the fullness of Christ?

His body. You are. I am. We are. We are all the fullness of Christ. We are a chip off the heavenly block. We reflect His very image and glory.

The New Testament model of ministry, birthed in Jerusalem, expanded to Antioch and perfected in Ephesus, is to be the pattern for church development today. God's plan and intention from the beginning was for all of mankind to carry His image and likeness so that we might rule together within His Kingdom. We know for certain that Christ is returning for His Church, a Church without spot or wrinkle. He will return in power and glory to establish His earthly Kingdom and rule and reign here on Earth. He has so chosen that we are to rule and reign with Him. Though the Kingdom of God is not fully established, it was begun when Christ came and will continue to expand until the consummation of all things, that is, until the nations have been reached with His great Gospel.

It is inherent upon every church within the locality, in unison, to build according to biblical patterns. To train and disciple men and women to maturity, to fulfill the Great Commission is still our greatest responsibility. Jesus said we would go to the entire world and preach the Gospel. The Good News of salvation through Jesus Christ was not meant for our local community alone; God's intention is that the nations of the world would submit to His rulership and be discipled to maturity.

Thus, one of the goals for any given local church is to be an integrated community where black, white, Hispanic, Asian, and American Indian work and function together, setting aside different cultures for a greater purpose. The church that is fulfilling its destiny in God will be a multi-cultural church, following a multi-cultural pattern as seen in the churches at Antioch and Ephesus.

Paul understood that we need to follow a pure pattern. What he is praying for in Ephesians chapter one, reminding the disciples in the city of Ephesus, is that he wanted them to understand and follow the pattern that he had instilled in them. Paul knew, perhaps better than anyone, that if we would follow the pattern, over time, Kingdom growth results. The faithful application of these principles is the key to Supernatural Building.

This is the Supernatural Architecture that God intended.

Modern churches can devise various strategies, programs and plans, but ultimately, God's strategy is for everyone to win one, to disciple one, with a focus on training and equipping God's people, then releasing them into their gifting and calling to reach others for Christ. The purpose? To impart that same model to others, city-by-city, nation-by-nation, until the Lord returns for His Church.

EPHESUS — GOD'S SUPERNATURAL ARCHITECTURE IN SUMMARY

From the beginning, the plan and purpose of the Lord was to build His church with the assistance of fleshly men through supernatural power. The church in Jerusalem was supernaturally born, birthed under very specific and dynamic circumstances, a Jewish church under apostolic anointing. The first church had many of the wonderful components most church growth experts desire to see. Included in this was the power of God manifested in healing and miracles, fellowship of a high caliber, occurring spontaneously, with tremendous commitment, with sacrifice being a standard and wonder being the norm. How glorious it must have been, though it did not fulfill the mandate of the Lord to disciple the nations.

As we have seen, Antioch became the first phase of the international model. It began out of adversity, almost by accident, as the Hellenistic Jews began to preach to the Jews; the Greeks pressed into the Gospel almost uninvited. Barnabas followed the model he learned in Jerusalem, adding to it the dimensions of corporate prayer for Holy Spirit direction, with the raising up of leaders in five-fold ministry gifting to assume their purpose in the Church.

As powerful as these churches were, there was a component of the supernatural, but with limited design, or at least without knowledge, plan and strategy on the part of God's chosen leaders.

Then there was Ephesus.

Apollos Built

The church in Ephesus, founded by Apollos and matured by Paul, became the model church by design and the leading of the Holy Spirit. At Ephesus, Paul took all he had previously learned, under the direction of the Holy Spirit, and duplicated Antioch with even greater success. In Ephesus he amalgamates the Jesus model of intense training of the disciples with the dynamic power of the Holy Spirit and builds a church, which at the time of John's Revelation, was estimated by some to be over 250,000 strong.[9] Such was the impact of this work that all of Asia, as it was known at the time, was touched by the Gospel, where truly extraordinary miracles were witnessed.

Many years after Paul planted the church in the great city of Ephesus, and after placing Timothy over the church as its Bishop, Paul writes a letter, expressing his heart and providing a supernatural look at what the Lord had done and intended to do, not just in Ephesus, but for the entire

---

[9] Please see the afterward by Dr. Chant who presents a sobering view of our often evangelistic beliefs on church growth in his historical context.

Church of Jesus Christ. As we have already reviewed, we can see in the book of Ephesians some of the key ingredients to this supernatural work, and, from his description, today's leaders can receive a glimpse of God's plan for the ages.

The Plan

From the beginning it has always been redemption. The will of God has always been to raise up apostles and prophets to establish the foundation of the supernatural church, to provide a way of salvation to a lost and dying world. In the first chapter of Ephesians, Paul writes about this incredible mystery which should be plain for the disciple to see.

The Lord's plan was to choose mankind from the foundation of the world to be His sons (inheritors). To be adopted by God meant to be chosen above all the rest, even the natural (Israel), with an ultimate end of making us holy and blameless before the world and God. It was never because of our deserving it, but because of the kind intention of His will, or His choosing, that salvation has come to us. This could only occur through a blood sacrifice provided by Christ. Through His provision, forgiveness through His wonderful grace occurs.

The thing that must have surprised Paul, and remains a source of wonderment, is that the Lord also chose to include us in His plan, and for man to assist in the administration of His plan for time and eternity. All of history, all of life, was summed up in Christ. Since we, as His disciples are in Him, we are also rich inheritors of His grace, called to fulfill His work. He came to establish an administration, the Kingdom of God, and we as His leaders are to be a part of the working out of His plan, His administration.

Because of the blessing of this plan and the revealed mystery for the entire world to see (even principalities and powers viewed the triumphant Christ when He arose from the grave), Paul focused his energy on the Church in all its problems and glory. For as unlikely as the institution seems at times to be, it is the divine instrument for the perfecting of the saints and the evangelizing of the world.

Paul, in his concern for the Church, prayed for it with great fervor. In verses 16-23 of chapter one, he expresses his concerns through his prayers. There was much that Paul could have prayed for, but his consuming passion was the Church, and God's people within its ever-expanding walls. He prayed for the Holy Spirit to provide supernatural wisdom to know the Lord without a mask or veil. The eyes of the Church needed to remain open, the heart clear, to fully comprehend the importance of the Church, our specific calling within it, and the rich and glorious inheritance which the believer was to walk in daily. More than the sweet by-and-by, the here-and-now Kingdom of God was Paul's concern, and the expansion of the Kingdom was the burden of his heart.

From a thorough understanding of the plan and purpose of the Logos of God flows the power of God. The resurrection power was meant for us to share...it has and always will be the source of witnessing, and the calling card of the Kingdom (signs and wonders). Those in the Church understood that truly the Earth would be filled with the knowledge of the glory of the Lord as the waters of the sea (Hab. 2:14). The Church would have access to supernatural power, and through the authority and the power of the Church in action, the supernatural architecture would develop.

More important than these actual steps to success was the knowledge of God's purposes, which would ignite the true believer to passion and action. It would move a prejudice believer to the embracing of the beautiful differences in the Kingdom. The understanding of the architectural and operational plan (the gifts, the five-fold ministry being used to equip the saints for service), included the importance of living free from any tie that binds, and to be a part of a sanctified community of believers where even the relationships would be transformed. They would be filled with love and mutual submission to prepare to defeat the principalities and powers and establish the Kingdom of Heaven on Earth.

Paul understood the mystery because he followed the pattern. Paul, in his life and ministry, more than any other, followed the pattern of the ages to reach, teach and release God's people through relational discipleship.

No other model will truly bring biblical results. Though numbers may increase and budgets may grow, unless men and women are being born-again by the Spirit of God, nurtured in loving community, trained and educated to maturity, and released into their highest gifting, what other activities we do may be good but they are not the Church. The Church of Jesus Christ has always existed, and will continue to grow and thrive in spite of what mankind might do.

The good ideas of man have often run contrary to the God ideas of the Lord found in His Word.

The hope of the Church is the emergence of the apostolic, with the gifting to set in order the house of the Lord, to rebuild the ancient foundations. It is the time of the Ephesus church, an emerging and mature Church that will again influence cities and nations for the Kingdom, and will by its very nature assist in the ushering in of the return of Christ.

This is the hope of the Church.

May His Kingdom come, may the apostolic emerge, and may the knowledge of the glory of the Lord continue to flow over the whole earth, as the supernatural architecture called the Church explodes.

END OF CHAPTER QUESTIONS

CHAPTER THIRTEEN

1. How does a church determine its ultimate vision? Who receives the vision? Can anyone in the church receive the vision from God, or is it just those in leadership?
2. Is giving responsibility to someone who doesn't think they are ready for it a good idea?
3. How could you recognize potential leaders? How do you know when they have been tested adequately?
4. How would you develop a leadership/discipleship program for the church?
5. Discuss some of the Jewish roots of Christianity. Why are they important to know and understand?
6. What is the priority of ministry as found in the New Testament?
7. How was Paul trained for ministry?
8. When is it appropriate to leave the local body to be trained elsewhere?
9. How could you establish solid foundational training in a formal setting without burdening the body further?

Chapter Fourteen

The Church of the 21st Century

Whenever a dissertation or a major thesis is written, there is normally a chapter included (chapter five in a standard research-oriented dissertation) called "Recommendations for Further Research." It is in this final chapter where the author, who has spent copious amounts of time and energy to justify a hypothesis, now has an opportunity to express what he/she really thinks and feels based upon the research conducted. In essence, this last chapter is very much like my recommendations for further research. It is my hope that this book thus far has not been as dry as most dissertations. But, it is essential that we look to the future of what the Church will hopefully become as we return to biblical roots and begin to apply them within cultural context.

As we come to the end of the 20th Century, we begin to focus with great anticipation on the 21st Century and all that implies. During this natural time of evaluation and transition, it behooves leaders within the Body of Christ to garner the mind of Christ and reevaluate the direction for the church of the locality. The decisions made and changes wrought will determine, to a great extent, the effectiveness of the Church of Jesus Christ over the next decade or two, should the Lord not return. Thus, with a hope towards being helpful, as well as to provide some apostolic and prophetic foundation for the 21st Century, this last chapter is presented.

To understand where we need to go, it is important to review where we are today. My critique, some would say criticism, of the modern Church needs to be kept within perspective. God is using many varied vehicles to reach the masses for the Lord Jesus Christ. All believers should rejoice in whatever manner a person experiences the saving knowledge of Christ. But just because someone comes to know the Lord through a certain methodology does not mean that it is the best way, or even a necessarily biblical way for us to reach the world for Christ. My perspective on this will become evident as we discuss some of the problem areas found within the modern-day Church, along with some of the corrections necessary to see God's purposes fulfilled.

Initially we will look at some of the dysfunctional components of the Church in the 20th Century that hopefully will not be carried into the Church of the 21st Century. These include the three schisms presented by Dr. Kirby Clemens at a recent Network for Christian Ministries meeting, along with two others, which divide. These five primary "isms" include Syncretism, Sexism, Racism, Denominationalism and Individualism. Each one is briefly covered here.

SYNCRETISM: A SPIRITUAL BLENDER

The first issue we will discuss is syncretism.

Syncretism is defined as "to attempt to blend and reconcile, as various philosophies" (*Funk and Wagnall's Encyclopedic Dictionary*). It speaks of the continuous effort to blend modern cultural trends or native religion with historic Christianity. There is no question that the Gospel must be contextualized to our present generation. However, to contextualize the Gospel does not mean that we must give up the basic tenets of the Gospel, or limit its most important and preeminent tool for reaching the lost...preaching the Word of God.

It is an unfortunate reality that many churches have attempted to become so "user-friendly" that they present a watered-down Gospel which is nothing more than a social message of love and caring for the neighbors in their community. Pluralism and humanism have certainly come into the Church, and we must continuously be on guard for such encroachments into the life of the Church that Christ established. The historical foundations for the Church must be recovered. Some of these foundational principles will be discussed in the next section. We must recognize that contextualization or even cultural adaptation and syncretism are not synonymous terms.

To syncretize the Gospel means to accept and accommodate aspects of culture to more easily win people to our belief system of Christianity. The methodology of assimilating aspects of culture to make Christian beliefs more palatable to the populace has been effectively utilized by the Roman Catholic Church from the earliest times. However, it is essential that we recover the pure Gospel of Christ, recognizing the need to develop worship services, programs and evangelistic outreaches that will be user-friendly in the positive sense. Our presentation of the Gospel must be presented in relevant and persuasive ways without compromising the essence of the message. Christ came to make disciples of the nations, not converts to a certain religious ethos. A true conversion experience will eventuate a different person, with a demonstrable difference seen between a Christian and being an American or any other nationality. This problem will have to be addressed by the emerging leadership of the 21st Century.

Sexism: Female leaders?

The second issue to be confronted (at least in America) is that of sexism.

It is amazing to me how the Church continues to battle over the usage and placement of women within the Church. The world, by-and-large, resolved this problem many years ago. They recognized that women who have talents and gifts should have every opportunity to express them to the best of their ability. There are very few limits on what a powerful woman of God can accomplish.

Often I am asked the question, "Dr. Stan, can a woman preach?" My response is: "It depends. It depends on if she is called to preach and if she is anointed to do so."

The same answer would be true for a man.

The real question is, "Should women have a place in government within the local church, in terms of the ordained office of elder or pastor?" This debate has gone on for centuries, and most likely will continue to be a controversial topic. It is my hope that the leadership of the 21st Century will be willing, through dialogue and prayer, to seek a clear understanding and revelation on the intent of scripture for the place of women in rulership or government.

It has been my experience that there are women who seem to go against the common understanding. That is, they have an incredible ability to lead congregations, even movements, with the highest level of expertise. Whether they are called a bishop, pastor, an apostle or prophet, they carry the ability to function in five-fold ministry authority. Further, to the dismay of many male leaders, they seem to function extremely well.

Are these women mere exceptions, or is this part of the grace of God in the New Testament Church? Must we necessarily, in the 21st Century, place limits on over 50% of the churches' labor force? These questions will need to be resolved by the leadership of the 21st Century.

The Racism Scourge

The third concern for 21st Century leaders is the insidious scourge of racism.

Unlike the church in most of Europe, the American church continues to struggle with this potentially explosive issue. Sunday morning is the most segregated day of the week! It is an offense to most leaders on the cutting-edge of what God is doing today to talk about a black church, or a white church, or an Hispanic church, or an Asian church.

Is Christ divided?

Of course not!

There is only one Church, the Church of Jesus Christ, which is visible here in the earth. As such, the Church should be as multi-cultural as possible. Each local church should be inclusive of every race, creed and color represented in its community. For every nation under the sun has a purpose in the divine mosaic of God.

Racism must be faced head on! If found in our hearts as white Americans, we must confess it and repent. If found in the heart of a person of color, the same response should be given. Beyond words of contrition and conciliatory rhetoric, there must be the fruit of repentance seen in inclusive relationships without limitations.

There is no superior race!

All of us have the same blood flowing through our veins — the blood of the Lord Jesus Christ. The Church must be willing to face the issue of racism, bring reconciliation where required, and begin the process of networking together with the "haves and the have nots", the powerful and the powerless, all working to fulfill the purposes of God.

Racism is a terrible disease in America. The love of God and the willingness of God's leaders to not just talk about reconciliation, but to actually reconcile, can eradicate this embarrassing condition of the heart.

DENOMINATIONALISM: DRAIN OR GAIN?

The fourth area of concern is denominationalism.

C. Peter Wagner has made a very powerful statement, referred to earlier, that the Church has entered a post-denominational reformation, a New Apostolic Reformation. He recognizes a new type of church emerging that is closer in affinity to the New Testament mode of church life and government. That is, anointed men/women of God have been used by the Lord to establish churches, to train believers, to raise up new works that are then subsequently planting churches throughout their community and around the world.

These new churches do not fit into a standard denominational structure. Denominations generally have a vast hierarchy with layers of administration which must be cared for and nurtured. Instead of the funds and other resources of the local church being used to support denominational structures, they are used for local church growth in the Kingdom.

Some of these outreaches, frankly, are self-centered and self-absorbed. Rather than being motivated by the Great Commission to take the Gospel to the nations, many independent churches, which are a part of a New Apostolic movement, are myopic at best. Most, if not all, of their money is kept for their own programs. Their concept of missions is simply to send their pastor on a two-week vacation to another part of the world to preach the Gospel. Though an exciting adventure, this approach leaves no permanent remnant of God's resources from the United States or another Western nation in an emerging Two-Thirds country. Again, denominationalism and its stranglehold upon the resources of God's people must be dealt with in the 21st Century as New Apostolic networks begin to grow, even within the midst of existing denominations.

INDIVIDUALISM

The fifth issue to be addressed, and perhaps the most insidious problem, or ism, of our day is that of individualism.

I hear people talk about an independent church, or with great pride state "I am an independent minister." I have difficulty seeing Christ accepting this concept, let alone the Apostle Paul.

What do they mean by independent?

Within American political history, rugged individualism and independence are words that we strongly embrace. We hold them dear as though they were Gospel themselves. The reality is, when Christ died for us, He died for our entire community. When we received Christ, we joined a greater community called the Body of Christ, expressed in and through local congregations around the world. Each congregation is to be individually governed by leadership within that local church, normally pastors, elders and deacons. But, each local church must be somehow connected to a larger body within their locality. This later connectedness is called "the church of the city" or the "church of the locality."

THE CITY CHURCH

Colin Dye, in his book, *Building a City Church* (Kings Way Publication, Dove Well Publication, Kensington Park Road, London, WII3BY, 1993), has stated that there are three elements to a city church:

1. A city church is organized into smaller, fully-functioning, self-contained and integral units. In common understanding, these would be called congregations with appropriate pastoral leadership.

2. These smaller units of the city church are recognizable as part of a larger whole. That is, they all fit together for greater purposes.

3. All Christians move and act together as a body to reach the city, warring against dogmatics or personal interpretations of scripture which divide and tend to conquer.

The city church is truly an apostolic church. It has a foundation established by its leadership that includes conversion from sin and repentance from dead works and iniquity. It has faith established in the heart, baptism in all of its dimensions, and all the basic understandings of the Word of God that need to be taught or imparted into the lives of believers. The individual church is often disconnected from the greater Body of Christ, which means it will loose its power and effectiveness due to being disconnected from the larger power source of the church of the city.

God is calling men and women around the world to develop this greater concept of a city church, a model of which is presented in the appendix of this book. A city church cares for, networks with, and develops programs and strategies for the greater Body of Christ, to reach their local community for the Lord. Further, it is a dynamic unit, working together to plant churches, establish missions and support existing works around the world.

In the 21st Century, it is vital that the leadership of the Body of Christ face and deal with the isms of the Church. We must prepare ourselves, our hearts, our minds and our spirits for the work that God has intended for us to do, which is to win the nations and disciple them to Christ.

The Apostolic Family:

The Church as the Family of God

It was the Apostle Paul who first developed the metaphorical teaching calling the Church a family. If we are going to understand the Church of the 20th Century and prepare the Church for the 21st, we must view the Church as a very large, extended family.

According to scripture, Christ is the head of the Church. The Holy Spirit is the one empowering and administrating the Church in the earth. The Father is the ultimate overseer of all things and all creation. If we are going to understand what is happening within the Church, we must be willing to conduct an analysis of the state of the family of God as it exists today. A diagnosis must be done, not a clinical diagnosis, but a differential or descriptive one, providing a picture of where the Church is and what things need to change. We must be willing to conduct an analysis of the state of the family of God as it exists today.

We must develop a treatment plan for the restoration of the Church. As most leaders will clearly agree, though the Church is still the most wonderful and precious instrument of the grace of God here in the earth, it is nonetheless dysfunctional in many ways. The Church needs healing and restoration.

God is calling on the five-fold ministry, especially apostles and prophets, to emerge and begin the work of setting again the proper foundation, of bringing correction as necessary to the Church, the Body of Christ.

Finally, we need a realistic prognosis for the future. We know that ultimately the Lord is building His church, a Church without spot or wrinkle. He has birthed a glorious Church, a bride prepared for His coming.

As we look at the Church, what things can be readily seen?

On a positive note, we see the Church growing at a faster rate now than ever before in history. There are more people being saved, sanctified and filled with the Holy Spirit today than at any other time, on either a per capita or a percentage basis, since the dawn of the Church age. We live in very exciting times. The focus of much of this evangelism is in the Two-Thirds world. Very little true growth is occurring in Europe, North America, Australia, or the other more "civilized" nations of the world. Where revival fires burn brightest, where people are being saved and churches are being planted, is in the Two-Thirds world. Africa is no longer the Dark Continent, but is filled with the light and life of God. African churches are sending out numerous, self-supported missionaries to the nations. South America has had an incredible revival. Many South Americans are now missionaries to North America and other parts of the world. The same phenomenon seems to be happening in Eastern Europe and in certain parts of Asia.

Glory and honor to the Lord should be given for these wonderful things. However, our concern must be for the continuation of a revival which can only come through discipleship, training and strategic planning. The truth is that the vast majority of the resources that are desperately needed to disciple the nations and to bring them into conformity with the will and purpose of God are maintained within Western nations. Churches throughout the United States, Canada, Australia and the United Kingdom have, by and large, focused their attention on themselves. It is exciting to see renewal, along with the positive results, for people hungry for God. Many have received restoration and healing.

Unfortunately, so much of the recent "times of refreshing" have resulted in immature and self-centered responses. "Give me more, Lord" is one of the phrases frequently heard, a far cry from the revivals of the past where the focus was on our responsibilities in the Gospel rather than our personal needs. To the people who are saying, "Lord, give me more," I would ask, "What about your neighbor? What about the nations?"

God's mandate for the Church will not be fulfilled through a consumption orientation. The Word of God states that Christians have already received all blessings in Christ. Our personal blessings are secondary. It is the blessing of the nations and the reaching of the lost that is our (and God's) primary concern.

In the Western church and many para-church movements, an incredible waste of resources is evident. It grieves my heart to see hundreds of thousands, even millions of dollars raised through Christian media events, such as through television, radio and even local church congregations, with a primary purpose of perpetuating that organization. They say, "I come to you today on TV Broadcast XYZ and I am asking you for money so that I can come again to you tomorrow on TV program XYZ. Tomorrow I will come to you and plead, cajole (some even manipulate) for the same thing, so I can come again the next day and do it all again." This cycle of fund-raising for the sake of fund-raising may not be the motivation of the heart of those involved, but it certainly detracts from the primary purpose of Christ.

In reality, most churches are not having primary growth, that is, growth that comes through evangelism. True evangelistic outreach results in new converts being added to the church, and would no doubt lead to the building of buildings or the finding of additional resources. However, most churches that are growing do so through transfer growth, which means luring people from one church to your church. This growth is attracted by various means, including styles of worship that "tickle the fancy" of the Western populace, or by providing unique programs that will meet the "felt needs" of the community.

I certainly have no problem with meeting the felt needs of people, but I am more concerned about meeting the real needs. These needs are the spiritual, social, even physical needs of the communities that we live in, which should by all means be addressed where possible. However, to address the real human needs of a community will take more than an individualistic approach. It will not happen through various media methods, although we thank God for what good some of them do. True and lasting change for a community will come as a result of a concerted and sustained effort under the authority of apostolic and prophetic men and women, working in concert for the greater purposes of God. Merely providing the best entertainment for the community during Christmas or Easter will not build Jesus' Church, though it may indeed attract a crowd. Hopefully the Church of the 21st Century will want more than the froth and bubble of experience, or crowds at the expense of the witness of Christ.

As we diagnose the Church, we must acknowledge that there are leaders with a primary orientation toward their own self-promotion, "taking care of number one." Obviously and thankfully they are a minority. The vast majority of five-fold ministry leaders and elders within local churches have one thing in mind: to see Jesus exalted. They are doing their best to bring people to Christ and glory to Him. It is unfortunate that those who are skirting standard methods of evangelism or doing sensational activities for the sake of activity are often brought to the forefront, presented as examples of true Christianity.

I believe that in the 21st Century we will not see a revival of superstars or of the great healing evangelists, although healing, miracles, etc., will be vital in reaching the lost for Christ. Miracle evangelism is part of the Supernatural Church. The future Church will be led by no-names that carry His name, empowered by the Holy Spirit, equipped by His ambassadors, released into their giftings for the cause of the Kingdom.

What then is the prognosis for the future?

My prognosis is positive.

Yes, there are major problems within the Church that must be addressed. We need to find ways to redistribute the wealth from Western nations to the world in need. We must find or develop programs and services that will equip God's people for full and effective ministry. This equipping is not to merely teach them how to give their tithes and offerings and live in comfortable, prosperous lifestyles. The equipping needed will, by design, prepare God's people to become everything that He intended for them to be. The laity must be released into effective service to win the world for Christ in our generation.

Further, we must see the emergence of true prophetic and apostolic ministry. Through the prophet, vision will be spoken into the lives of people. The Church in the city will become sensitive to the voice of the Lord, becoming a city of refuge and a shelter for the lost. We need to have the apostolic foundations established. These foundations will include those presented at the church in Jerusalem, where they received apostolic and prophetic instruction, broke bread, fellowshipped in intimate relationships, had praise and worship as earmarks of their lifestyle, with evangelism as their focus (Acts 2:42, 46-47).

In addition to these foundation stones will be the Antioch church dynamics of the five-fold ministry emerging in the city church with special times of intense prayer and fasting to clearly hear a word from God. There will be a willingness to overcome cultural differences, being filled with generosity for the sake of the Gospel, and an understanding of the Great Commission to disciple the nations by sending the very best (Acts 11:19-30; 13:1-4).

Finally, where inadequate doctrine or experience was found, all was set in order. The foundation stones of a healthy family — baptism, the gifts in operation, and teaching for transformation of character and purpose — were emphasized, and the Supernatural Church was launched (Acts 19:1-20).

Through the apostle, the purposes of the Church can be established. The Church is to be a place where the lost can be won, the broken healed, the misguided set back on course, and where men and women who had little or no purpose can find their place in God's economy. The apostle and prophet must learn to work together with the rest of the five-fold ministry and the Church-at-large as companies effecting communities for good.

Leaders will set appropriate goals for a city, based upon a life of prayer and mutual accountability. Not unity for the sake of unity, but unity for the sake of purpose, establishing proper government within local communities based upon principles of Kingdom living. These are essential, as are plans that are birthed in corporate prayer where our work can be lovingly brought into the light of mutual relational accountability. Leaders in the 21st Century will no longer be doing their own individualistic thing, but will willingly set aside personal programs for the greater good of the Body of Christ.

For the necessary changes to occur, leaders around the world must be willing to face the truth. Each of us have been raised in a form of dysfunctional family. None of us have a perfect model of church family life. All of us have been affected to one extent or another by the craziness of the Church of the 20th Century. We should not deny it, but embrace the truth and bring it into the light — not the light of the media, but the light of the Word of God — as we gather as God's ambassadors to grapple with our identity and purpose.

It is not too late for us to repent, to seek answers, to have our relational sins forgiven, to determine within our hearts to work together with men and women of like precious faith for the greater purposes of God.

I, for one, am tired of Church as we have seen it. I am longing for the Supernatural Church God intended, summarized best in the church in the city of Ephesus. One last time I return to the book of Acts to see the results of the pattern established by the Apostle Paul in this great church.

In the 19th chapter of the book of Acts, the Apostle Paul finds believers in the city of Ephesus. Once found, he immediately determined their foundation. "How were you saved? Were you baptized in water? Were you baptized in the Holy Spirit? Are you free to operate in the gifts of the Spirit?" Paul made sure he knew what the true needs of these saints were before proceeding, for these things were absolutely vital. He knew that before any real teaching could begin, he must know who they were in Christ. Their experiences in Christ had to be completed with baptisms that would identify them to the Church and fill them with the empowerment of the Holy Spirit, necessary ingredients for effective living.

The Apostle Paul dealt with first things first.

He did not set his attention on church growth, on building acquisition, or even on evangelism. He set his heart, as Jesus did, on the equipping of the twelve and the others that would follow after them, to prepare them for ministry. In the 8th verse of chapter 19 we see Paul enter the synagogue and begin to teach about the Kingdom of God. The religious leadership, as was common, rejected him, so he established a school of ministry for the city. The school of Tyrannous, likely a rented facility for children or adults, was used to begin the process of teaching disciples, a repeat of previously learned and tested patterns. Paul trained and taught the converts in that city, both Jews and Greeks, all that he had received from Jesus and all he had learned with Barnabas. It was multi-cultural ministry, the only way Paul would have it.

After two years of intense instruction, likely filled with a mixture of the theological and practical, growth of the church began to occur. The result of the teaching ministry, after having laid an appropriate foundation for the disciples, was that extraordinary miracles began to manifest. Deliverance from demonic oppression occurred. People who had debilitating diseases were miraculously healed.

In the ministry of Peter, his mere shadow, when it crossed over someone, would instantaneously and miraculously heal and deliver. How much more extraordinary must have been the miracles through Paul. From these miracles, and from Paul sending out teams into the outlying areas, comprised of students he had trained, the Gospel of the Kingdom reached Asia Minor. People were being saved, churches were being planted, revival fires were lit throughout that region and into regions beyond.

What does God want to do through us in the 21st Century?

It will take an Ephesus-type of ministry to produce His Supernatural Church. It is God's intention to restore back the full functioning of the church of the city, where His purposes for the nations are accomplished. Our purpose is to effectively and completely equip God's people in preparation for the promised revival. God will allow us to choose from a variety of models and methods to complete the task. Each community will need unique approaches, to be discovered by the respective leaders within that given community. However, the primary goal must remain the same: our primary responsibility must flow with the general patterns of scripture. For some communities, a cell-based church model will be best. In others, it may be a megachurch that will get the job done. In other places, standard local churches planted on every street corner throughout the world will be the plan (this is by far the best).

All I really know is this — if we catch the vision of what God intends to do, our hearts and minds will change. Our focus will no longer be on our own programs or ourselves, but we will be intently determined to find and do the will and purpose of God for the expansion of His Kingdom in the earth. I long for the 21st Century Church to be different than what we've experienced in the 20th. I thank God for every great warrior of the cross of Christ that has come before us and has laid a foundation stone to the church of the city. Of course, we must take the time to do a painstaking analysis of our lives and ministries, willing to evaluate what has gone before, not throwing the baby out with the bath water but changing the dirty water where needed. It is time for leaders in the Body of Christ to look towards the 21st Century, not settling for church as usual, but seeking instead to settle for nothing less than His Supernatural Church!

In the 21st Century Church, growth and development will occur because of the empowerment of the Holy Spirit through yielded servants of God. The Lord will use for His purposes trained, equipped and empowered laity who will go into the highways and byways and compel men and women to come in, led by apostolic and prophetic teams, discipling the nations until the Lord returns. We are building for the next generation, a generation who will fulfill the mandate for the Church.

> *"Listen, O my people, to my instruction; Incline your ears to the words of my mouth. I will open my mouth in a parable; I will utter dark sayings of old, Which we have heard and known, and our fathers have told us. We will not conceal them from their children, but tell to the generation to come the praises of the Lord, and His strength and His wondrous works that He has done. For He*

established a testimony in Jacob, and appointed a law in Israel, which He commanded our fathers, that they should teach them to their children, That the generation to come might know, even the children yet to be born, that they may arise and tell them to their children, That they should put their confidence in God, but keep His commandments, And not be like their fathers, a stubborn and rebellious generation, a generation that did not prepare its heart, and whose spirit was not faithful to God" (Psalm 78:1-8 NAS).

END OF CHAPTER QUESTIONS

CHAPTER FOURTEEN

1. Describe some characteristics unique to the church in Ephesus. How different is this church growth strategy from your church?
2. List from your perspective some of the key problems found in the Church at large.
3. If you could make any changes within your church structure, what would they be and why.

Afterward

All discussion on the growth patterns of the Church needs to take into account the experience of the apostolic churches. People often have an idealized and unrealistic view of the early Church, and of the rate of its worldwide expansion. In fact, it is likely that by the year 100 the total number of Christian converts was scarcely as many as 20,000. Even 200 years after the day of Pentecost, the number of Christians in the Roman Empire probably did not exceed 2% of the population. By the year 300, that figure had increased to about 10%.

This parallels the growth of the Pentecostal movement in our time, which some say now embraces about 200 million people. This, after 200 years of witness, represents 3% of the world's present population. So if the early Church may be taken as a reasonable guide, we have no need to hang our heads low!

Ancient sources suggest that across the first 250 years (until the time of Constantine), and despite persecution, the Church increased by about 40% every decade. After the conversion of Constantine, the Church multiplied even more. By the middle of the 4th Century, Christians probably numbered more than half of the population of the empire; some parts of the empire were totally Christian.

That slow, though steady, expansion should cool the wilder expectations of church growth in our own time. The path of wisdom is surely to not expect too much or too little growth. To anticipate more than is sensible is to court disillusionment; to anticipate less than scripture and history encourage is to grieve the Holy Spirit.

During the first 250 years, converts were less seldom made in large numbers at one time, nor did the labors of the Christian apologist persuade more than a few to abandon paganism. Local congregations across that period rarely numbered more than a handful of people, and they lacked the resources to mount great evangelistic endeavors. For nearly three centuries, the growth of the Church occurred without mass crusades, revivals, big name preachers, user-friendly churches, growth strategies, plans, techniques and other methods — that is, without any of the things that are today commonly thought essential!

Rather, people were added to Christ...

By the steady witness of individual Christians,

By the example the believers gave of Christian love and charity,

By planting local churches,

And occasionally, by unusually successful missions conducted by itinerant preachers.

Further, the "easy-believism" common today was almost unknown during those first centuries. In most churches, neophytes had to undergo instruction for three years or more before they were allowed baptism and given admittance to the Eucharist.

It is worth noting, too, that during the persecutions that occurred across the first 300 years, the total number of martyrs was not large, certainly no more than several thousand. Indeed, some historians think the number should be expressed in hundreds. Usually, the church leaders were arrested, and only occasionally were the ordinary members of local churches in any peril of arrest or torture. Since this 20th Century of ours has seen more martyrs for Christ than in all the previous centuries combined, the significant growth the Church is presently enjoying worldwide is all the more remarkable.

I am inclined to think that the churches identified as "New Apostolic Churches," when stripped of their 20th Century trappings and style, are not very much different from church groups in the past. For example, in the United Kingdom, from the late 16th to the late 17th centuries, there was a situation similar to our own time. Scores of enthusiastic, independent churches and groups of churches sprang up, some with outlandish names, full of fiery zeal, and perfectly persuaded that they were signs of the Second Coming of Christ. They included different styles of church government, and many claimed an apostolic identity. In the end, they either perished, or were absorbed back into the handful of mainline denominations that survived the horrors of the English Civil War.

One hundred years later England and North America were shaken by the Wesleyan revivals. Those early Methodists were also convinced that the return of Christ was at hand — were they not a witness of that great approaching day? They too saw themselves as shaking off the dead yoke of the old denominationalism, and had characteristics similar to the brash young churches of our time. For example, here is how Charlotte Brontë describes a meeting in a Wesleyan chapel in Yorkshire, during the first decade of the 19th century, less than twenty years after the death of John Wesley - [10]

Briar Chapel, a large, new, raw Wesleyan place of worship, rose but a hundred yards distant; and, as there was even now a prayer meeting being held within its walls, the illumination of its windows cast a bright reflection on the road, while a hymn of a most extraordinary description, such as a very Quaker might feel himself moved by the Spirit to dance to, roused cheerily all the echoes of the vicinage. The words were distinctly audible by snatches: here is a quotation or two from different strains; for the singers passed jauntily from hymn to hymn and from tune to tune, with an ease and buoyancy all their own.

> *Oh! who can explain*
> *This struggle for life,*
> *This travail and pain,*
> *This trembling and strife?*
> *Plague, earthquake, and famine,*

---

[10] <u>Shirley</u>, Chapter Nine, "Briarmains."

> And tumult and war,
> The wonderful coming
> Of Jesus declare!
>
> For every fight
> Is dreadful and loud, -
> The warrior's delight
> Is slaughter and blood;
> His foes overturning,
> 'Til all shall expire, -
> And this is with burning,
> And fuel, and fire!

Here followed an interval of clamorous prayer, accompanied by fearful groans. A shout of "I've found liberty! Doad o' Bill's has found liberty!" rung from the chapel, and out all the assembly broke again.

> What a mercy is this!
> What a heaven of bliss![11]

The stanza which followed this, after another and longer interregnum of shouts, yells, ejaculations, frantic cries, agonized groans, seemed to cap the climax of noise and zeal.

> Sleeping on the brink of sin,
> Tophet gaped to take us in;
> Mercy to our rescue flew, -
> Broke the snare and brought us through.
> Here, as in a lion's den,
> Undevour'd we still remain;
> Pass secure the watery flood,
> Hanging on the arm of God.
> Here —the roof of the chapel did not fly off;
> which speaks volumes in praise of its solid slating.

---

[11] The remainder of this stanza, plus three others, are then given in the book.

Afterward

Later in the same work, Charlotte Brontë imagines Caroline searching for something to read and coming across... *"some mad Methodist magazines, full of miracles and apparitions, of preternatural warnings, ominous dreams, and frenzied fanaticism."* [12]

Dr. Ken Chant
President, Vision Christian College of Australia

---

[12] Chapter Twenty Two, "Two Lives."

Supernatural Architecture

APPENDIX

APPENDIX 1

VISION INTERNATIONAL NETWORK OF MINISTERS AND MINISTRIES

CITY CHURCH NETWORK (CCN)[13], A MODEL

THE APOSTOLIC MOVEMENT

The great Christian movements of the past have served a vital purpose in their time to move the Church forward toward the restoration of all things. With the restoration of the apostle, prophet, evangelist, pastor and teacher gifts of Ephesians 4, the Body of Christ is beginning to come to maturity. Only when the office of the apostle is restored can there be the fullness of Jesus the Apostle (Hebrews 3:1) within His people. The Church can never be considered completed or fully matured until we see a manifestation of apostles in the Church.

We live in a kairos time in human history, a time of transition. As we enter the 21st Century, the Church must be restored more fully to God's original intent if we are to fulfill the Great Commission and disciple the nations to the Lord Jesus Christ. This time of transition has been called "post-denominational" or "A New Apostolic Reformation." There needs to be a demonstration in this generation of the ministry of the apostle with power, not simply elegant words, if we are to see world-changing productivity. When apostles begin to arise by the thousands, the Church will be released

---

[13] I am indebted to Rev. George Runyan, Founder and Director of the San Diego City Church Network for allowing me to assist with and adapt this material from original brochures and booklets that describe this dynamic ministry.

to effectively disciple the nations who are willing to receive the Lordship of Christ.

The harvest cannot be brought in apart from this foundational office. In answer to the Spirit's cry to "restore," we are seeing the Father raise up a new generation of apostles and apostolic people to take their place in the earth, making their invaluable contribution to the work of God. This requires a fresh anointing and people who are willing to embrace something new while building on and cleaving to the landmarks and foundations of yesterday. It will require experienced men of anointing and integrity to set the pace for taking cities and nations as the early Church did in the first century, thus establishing Christ's dominion in the earth.

As part of this apostolic visitation, CCN has been formed to play a significant role in God's plan for His end-time people. Apostolic and prophetic leaders, both in this city and abroad, are uniting to plant and strengthen churches through this network of covenant relationships. CCN is birthed out of a commitment to serve the Body of Christ by bridging leaders and integrating missions in a biblical and meaningful way.

CCN is a movement of ministries dedicated to the church of the locality. The biblical model of the Church was addressed as the church in a locality (like Ephesus, Corinth, etc.), made up of God's redeemed people. The primary focus of the Network is to serve the individual congregations and their leadership.

For more information on recognized Apostolic Networks such as the San Diego City Church Network, please contact Vision, 940 Montecito Way, Ramona, CA 92065.

CCN's Vision

We believe the Lord is restoring to His Church the New Testament apostolic model of ministry. Three patterns of local church are seen in the New Testament: Jerusalem, Antioch and Ephesus. We believe that Ephesus is the pattern of church life in a locality. The church was noted for its plurality of elders giving care to the church and trans-local ministries like those of Apollos, Paul and Timothy spending time in Ephesus to plant and build the church of that locality. This was done with a view towards bringing the Church to maturity.

The church at Antioch (Acts 11-13) serves as a pattern for raising up apostolic ministry that is sent to plant and care for churches. The teaching and prophetic ministry are seen working in tandem to accomplish God's Kingdom purpose. It is at Antioch that Barnabas and Saul were called and sent as an apostolic team.

The Church is in an Antioch time. The teaching and prophetic ministries have been restored to the Church. The Church in this hour is being called to prayer and fasting. The apostolic ministry is just beginning to develop. There are many apostolic networks in the formative stage, being established throughout the Earth with a vision of training and sending. In the San Diego region, such a training center has been established known as the Vision International School of Ministry.[14]

THE PURPOSE OF CCN

For this purpose CCN is formed. The New Testament apostolic pattern revealed throughout the book of Acts shows two primary priorities in ministry: The first being that of the planting of indigenous churches in every locality as the Spirit directs. The second is the strengthening of those churches that have already been established, assisting them to conform to New Testament patterns.

---

[14] Vision International School of Ministry is a program of Vision International University, which has developed a network of Bible Colleges in over 90 nations of the world, offering degree granting and curriculum support for thousands of students worldwide.

CCN has adopted these priorities as its purpose for being. To plant and strengthen the church of the locality, CCN prioritizes the following four basic ministry vehicles, which when judiciously applied, will assist in the development of the church in the locality.

These include:

1. Leader-to-leader relationships, with a focus on building helpful and trusting relationships for the sake of the Body of Christ within the locality. This is best accomplished through weekly prayer meetings, frequent fellowship, and strategic networking of ministry in support of the greater vision for the city or region.
2. Church-to-church relationships, a natural extension of the development of trusting and mutually beneficial relationships amongst leaders. On a quarterly basis, joint ministry between and with different congregations within a city is conducted, thus breaking down barriers of potential jealousy and fear, while working together in areas of common need as a witness of the purpose of God for the region.
3. Trans-local ministry as it relates to the church of the locality, coordinating the ministry of known speakers and other ministry with the needs of the region, and sharing of resources once kept exclusively within a certain stream or denomination.
4. Conferences and training events designed to equip the larger Body of Christ within an area utilizing the giftedness of God's leaders already found in local assemblies. Many local churches are especially rich in personnel, some in areas of workers, and others with finances. All the Body of Christ is to work together for the greater good of the members, until all become fully mature

and released into their calling. A concerted and coordinated effort must be made to see this accomplished.

The Network of Churches, which are in relationship with one another, is building upon New Testament patterns of local and trans-local ministries. This includes a careful attempt to establish relationships with ministries of common vision, with a willingness to work in unified effort for the larger Body of Christ. Special care has been taken to conform to scriptural paradigms for ministry. These patterns translate within the Network to clearly established governmental structures as a framework for effective ministry. They include:

The CCN Structure

The Leadership Council

The Network is ultimately led by founding apostles and overseers; it is not governed by any one man. Instead, a council of mature, committed leaders, ministering in the capacity of the five-fold ministry gifts according to Ephesians 4:11, collectively represents VIN/CCN Fellowship of Ministries and Ministers.

Convening Councils

A convening council is based on an understanding of Acts 15, where the leaders of the Church gathered for serious dialog and problem resolution. Throughout Church history, councils have been convened as needed for similar purposes. Convening councils are part of the CCN government, designed to deal with regional and global ministry concerns.

APOSTOLIC COMPANY

The apostolic company refers to all ordained leaders within CCN. Those members are not a part of an exclusive club, but are a team of committed men and women who desire the benefit of the church in the locality above their own personal ministry. Thus, the company is developed by the knitting together of lives by the Holy Spirit, men and women who can in love work together for common goals. Generally, membership occurs by recommendation and always through relationship.

REGIONAL PRESBYTERIES

One of the essential keys to CCN is relationship. Presbyteries within CCN are local gatherings of ministries that function to build Network relationships. They are far more than the traditional ministerial association or fellowships, which may lead to carnal comparisons, empty agendas and needless frustration. True relationships within the presbytery provide the basis for growth and blessing within the Network, and translate to healthier teams and churches.

Presbyteries within the Network also provide relational opportunity and ministry for the pastors' spouses. This is accomplished by planning social events and structuring time at monthly presbytery meetings where relationships may develop. Presbyteries also provide a context for conferences, planting churches and the sponsoring of common trans-local events which connect the churches and ministries for mutual benefit.

CCN MISSIONS

The combined missions' strategy seeks to express the heart and mind of God for this moment in the end-time harvest. It is recognized that the local church is the foundational element for fulfilling the Great Commission. CCN is a facilitating agent that serves local churches in their desire to make a meaningful contribution to the evangelization of the world.

Some underlying principles which empower the missions approach include:

> Strong local churches
>
> Equipping the Body for Ministry
>
> Team Ministry
>
> Personal involvement within the Network Churches and Members
>
> Financial and Practical Accountability
>
> Indigenous Self Support
>
> Financial Synergism

How It Works

Each Network church is linked through prayer, finances and ministry teams to the missions the Network has chosen to support. A "mission" is considered anything outside the local congregation. These ministries are evaluated by the Leadership Council as to their compatibility with the Network's vision, standards of leadership, integrity and scriptural methodology. This provides for an extension of the Kingdom of God with accountability. Ministries may be adopted into the Network from Network churches upon verification of that ministry's compliance with Network criteria for support.

Apostolic Teams

Apostolic teams are sent to overseas ministries that are in relationship with CCN. Specifically, there must have been an advance team that has visited and recommended that particular ministry. An apostolic team's major purpose is to build and strengthen the local congregation and its leadership through leadership seminars, church-wide training, Bible College planting, and other ministry services. Their focus is to support the local leaders functioning in ministry to the community. Apostolic teams are selected by the Leadership Council from among ministers within the Network. Interested ministers will make themselves available for involvement at this level, as needed and as led by the Holy Spirit.

Prophetic Teams

The prophet is part of the apostolic team to envision and affirm leaders and individuals in their call. The prophets support the governmental responsibility of the apostolic team. They are vital to the ministry of the presbytery. The prophetic ministry will see in advance the vision of the Lord and/or confirm the direction the apostolic team is sensing to take.

Evangelistic Teams

Evangelistic teams work in relationship with national leaders and local pastors and their congregations. They have a three-fold purpose: training local church members in evangelism, strengthening national churches and evangelizing the lost directly.

Help Teams

Helps teams function under the leadership of the Network to assist in the construction of churches, schools, clinics and other projects. Because the very nature of CCN is apostolic, the missions portion of the work together is of

Appendix 1

the utmost priority. It is envisioned that an ever-increasing impact upon a city, nation and the nations will occur through the growth and strength of the Network. It is the heart of Vision International Network and the City Church Network.

Why should a minister be a part of a Network?

There are several important and related blessings from involvement within an Apostolic Network. They include:

1. The Blessing of Committed Relationships
2. The Blessing of Vision and Mission
3. The Blessing of Covering
4. The Blessing of Opportunity
5. The Blessing of Challenge
6. The Blessing of Synergy
7. The Blessing of Life

APPENDIX 2

GATHERING OF APOSTLES AND PROPHETS CONFERENCE 1996

In September of 1996, a historic conference was held at Fuller Theological Seminary under the leadership of Dr. C. Peter Wagner. The purpose of the conference was to discuss and present the concept of the Apostolic Network or Council of Apostles and Prophets. Some of the information from that conference is presented here with commentary by the author.

"We cannot establish apostolic anointing until we deal with fatherhood!"

"Cut out the old and establish the new."

"We need to be a loving-affirming-encouraging generation."

"The Church must repent of rejection and rebellion."

"Moves of the past have been birthed out of rejection."

These and other comments were made by, or in conjunction with, Dr. C. Peter Wagner — speaking from "The Conference for The New Apostolic Reformation" held at Fuller Theological Seminary, Pasadena, CA, 1996. Part of the theme for this conference can be summarized in the scripture provided below.

> *"Look among the nations! Observe! Be astonished! Wonder! Because I am doing something in your days—You would not believe if you were told"* (Habakkuk 1:5).

The decade of the 90's has become the greatest time of world harvest. Throughout the world, from many diverse

mission fields, outstanding manifestations of the Spirit of God in action have been seen. These include:
- Great spiritual manifestations, including millions of souls being won to Christ and outstanding miracles of healing.
- A move, or at least a sense of the need, for unity within the Body of Christ.
- The greatest prayer movement since the First Century Church has been and continues to be seen around the Earth.
- A powerful releasing of God's grace in the Third World, resulting in the greatest move of Christianity ever seen, especially in areas of:
  a. Leadership: Tremendous men and women of God have emerged from seemingly nowhere, leaders who are inordinately gifted with the power of God to work miraculous results and build the Church of Jesus Christ.
  b. Finances: Many formerly colonized and financially dependent nations are becoming self-sufficient, even becoming missionary by sending and supporting churches.

This is creating the most dramatic and meaningful change in the normal way of "doing church" since the Protestant Reformation, a move forward to the roots of the Apostolic church as outlined in the book of Acts.

In every continent of the world, a dynamic type of church growth is occurring that is leading the way!

The Root of growth can be seen in:
- Africa: Independent churches have been growing for over 100 years, beginning to leave behind the dependency on western support fostered by the policies of colonialism and racist control.

- The House Church Movement: Mainland China continues to boom, with an estimated 60 to 100 million believers actively worshipping under Communist repression.

- Grass roots churches: Throughout Latin America, these churches are being established almost daily, with tremendous expansion, primarily through the activation of lay leadership.

- In America, the fastest growing churches since the 80's are the Charismatic, independent congregations that emphasize the gifts of the Holy Spirit and personal evangelism.

These trends are continuing into the present time, resulting in a re-evaluation of the methodology for church growth in Western nations, and the discussion of a new "wine skin" for the new wine being manifested.

In this conference, the term "Apostolic Reformation" was used to describe a New Testament-patterned church which is actively sending men and women into the harvest field worldwide, with a focus on the restoration of the ministry of the apostle in and through churches within a locality.

TEN ASPECTS OF THE NEW APOSTOLIC CHURCHES

Within the conference there were ten aspects of the New Apostolic Churches noted. They are:

1. A new name - Apostolic Church
2. A New Authority: the amount of spiritual authority is primarily being delegated by the Holy Spirit to individuals over and against boards or denominational structures moving from having authority through legal structures alone to biblical forms of government with a change from external control (denominational) to consideration of local needs. A change from rational or political leadership

to charismatic leadership. The pastor is viewed as the leader instead of as an employee. The pastor's accountability is changing from the local church board to a plurality of elders and external presbytery leadership within the church, established for three reasons:

    a. You are my friend
    b. You agree with me
    c. You agree with the vision of this church

3. There is a new structure for the operation of the local church in terms of:
    a. Organization, becoming more theocratic than democratic or autocratic, functional, with the people doing the ministry, while pastors give up the active daily ministry in favor of prayer, the ministry of the Word and giving leadership to the people.
    b. Staffing: More and more are becoming home-grown, raised up from within the congregation through formal or informal structures of training and education. Thus, many are starting Bible Colleges within the local church to train leaders with a new vision imparted through the local leadership

4. A New Focus for ministry is emerging, from a traditional model, generally driven by the pastor and heritage, to a vision-driven ministry, lead by the Spirit of the Lord and biblical patterns.

5. A New Worship Style is coming to the forefront, with a major element of unity expressed in and through corporate worship which is participatory in focus, rather than performance-oriented. Instruments are used which are similar to music in society, yet used to bring praise and glory to the Lord. There is more creativity, including

dance, kneeling, raising hands, extended times in worship, which are spontaneous and dynamic.

6. New Prayer Forms are developing, to include movements such as Prayer 2000 and the Concerts of Prayer, and a movement of pastors and other leaders bowing in prayer for the benefit of the city is beginning to change the way ministers and ministries are relating to one another, for the benefit of the Kingdom of God.

7. New Financing is a part of this Reformation, including:
   a. Relatively few financial problems, with a recognition that part of Christian responsibility is tithing, thus...
   b. Greater resources for specific vision and missions are being made available.

8. New Outreaches are emerging; more apostolic in focus, with the word apostolic meaning "to reach the lost, be sent out" with the intention of church planting, church mission expansion and social service. These outreaches are local church directed and involve pastors taking teams to the nations to reach the world for Christ and provide resources to the nations for discipleship.

9. New Power Paradigms are evident, such as:
   a. Spiritual authority, or headship without domination.
   b. Spiritual fatherhood/mentoring, seen as a method of meeting the need to train, supervise and support the next generation of leaders.
   c. Apostolic company and councils are emerging around the world, networking ministries for common purpose.

10. Home Cell Groups are seen as a means of dynamic church growth, through providing both opportunities for ministry needs of the people to be met, and as a model for training and releasing the people of God into greater service for the Lord.

All ten of these relatively new and exciting developments seem to indicate a change in thinking and action is coming to the Church, which appears to be led by the Spirit of the Lord, Who is breathing new life into His Church. The new wine, as described by some, requires a new wine skin, or new paradigms which will allow for a fresh move of the Spirit of God without negating the continual need for consistent pastoral ministry, teaching of the Word of God in depth, and the disciplines of the Church which provide stability and growth for the future.

THE PRAYER TRACK FOR A.D. 2000

One of the most unique and outstanding aspects of the "New Apostolic Reformation" is the emphasis on prayer, both individual and corporate. One manifestation of this new prayer focus can be seen in the A.D. 2000 prayer movement. This movement emphasizes the need for prayer because so many exciting things are happening in the world that need to be covered in prayer.

The Church worldwide is in the midst of the greatest harvest the world has ever known. It is estimated that 140 thousand individuals are being born-again each day. The nation of the world having the greatest harvest is China — thirty-five thousand precious people a day are being born-again. This requires discipleship and leadership training, two of the primary needs of the nations.

The greatest supernatural outpouring the world has ever seen is also occurring in India, the greatest accessible country (to Western Missions). It also has about thirty-five thousand people a day giving their lives to Christ!

In Africa, twenty-thousand souls a day are being born-again (clearly, Africa is no longer to be considered the "dark continent"). South Africa, in one day, in one location, had a regional baptism of seventy-five thousand men, women and children!

Appendix 2

A Prayer army for the Muslims' salvation is occurring, including 2,000,000 prayer guides being printed — one for adults and one for children. Their prayer emphasizes a blessing — ask that God will bless their prayers to Him for they pray, "O God, please reveal Yourself to me!"

He is doing just that!

Divine visitations — mostly among the Muslims, are occurring as reported by missionaries around the world. Muslims are giving their hearts to Christ and are reporting many such manifestations.

Jesus said to pray. The apostles made prayer a center point of their ministry, and prayer is a powerful tool, the foundation of our relationship with Christ and the releasing of evangelism into the nations.

When Satan has people under his power, he never gives them up without a fight! Prayer is seen as one of the most powerful weapons for spiritual warfare. Though there are varied opinions on the importance and place of spiritual warfare, one thing is for certain: The Lord is calling His Church to prayer and the ministry of the Word in preparation for his end-time revival.

Bibliography

Burns, J. A. M. *Leadership*. New York: Harper and Row. 1978

Cairns, Earle E. *Christianity Through The Centuries: History of the Christian Church*. Grand Rapids: Zondervan. 1981.

DeArtega, William. *Quenching The Spirit*. Lake Mary: Creation House. 1992.

Demazio, Frank. *The Making Of A Leader*. Portland: Bible Temple Publishing. 1988

Greenway, Roser S. *Cities: Mission's New Frontier*. Baker Books. 1989

Haggai, John. *Lead On! Milton Keynes*. Word Publishing. 1986

McBirnie, William S. *The Search For The Early Church*. Wheaton: Tyndale House.

Mead, Frank S. Revised by Hill, Samuel S., *Handbook of Denominations In The United States*. Nashville: Abingdon Press. 1985.

Scheidler, Bill. *The New Testament Church And Its Ministries*. Portland: Bible Temple Publishing. 1980.

Wilson, Marvin R. *Our Father Abraham: Jewish Roots Of The Christian Faith.* Grand Rapids: Eerdmans Publishing Company. 1989.

Wagner, C. Peter. *Spiritual Power and Church Growth.*

Berger, Carl F. *How to Break Growth Barriers.*

McGavaran, Donald. *Understanding Church Growth.*

McGavaran and Winfield. *10 Steps For Church Growth.* Harper and Roc Pub. New York, New York, 1977

Recommended Resources

DeKoven, Stan E., *New Beginnings*, Vision Publishing.

DeKoven, Stan E., *Parenting on Purpose*, Vision Publishing.

DeKoven, Stan E., *On Belay!*, Vision Publishing.

Chant, Ken, *Better Than Revival*, Vision Publishing.

About the Author

Dr. Stan DeKoven is a licensed Marriage, Family and Child Counselor in California, working for many years in the field. He is the Founder and President of Vision International Ministries, with programs including Vision International University and Vision Bible College, Network of Campuses worldwide, Vision Publishing, The American Society of Christian Therapists and the Family Care Network. He is the author of over 30 books in practical Christian living for the maturing of God's people.

OTHER BOOKS BY DR. DEKOVEN

Family Violence: Patterns of Destruction

I Want to Be Like You Dad:
Breaking Free from Generational Patterns
— Restoring the Heart of the Father

Leadership: Vision for the City

Journey to Wholeness
Marriage and Family Life

Pastoral Ministry

Turning Points

For scheduling Dr. DeKoven, or for book orders, contact:

VISION PUBLISHING
940 MONTECITO WAY
RAMONA, CA 92065

1-800-9VISION

(760) 789-3023 FAX

www.viu.com